WHERE FREEDOM BEGINS
The Process of Personal Change

WHERE FREEDOM BEGINS

The Process of Personal Change

Marion Pastor, Ph.D. &
Ron Luyet, M.F.C.C., M.A.

WINGBOW PRESS, OAKLAND

Wingbow books are published and distributed by Bookpeople, 7900 Edgewater Drive, Oakland, California 94621

Manufactured in the United States of America.
Designed by Mark Anderson/Boilerplate
Cover Photos by Superstock (Family), Joanie Pacheco/Boilerplate (Woman)
Printed by Walsworth Publishing

ISBN: 0-914728-79-2

First Wingbow Edition, Winter 1993

Pastor, Marion
Where Freedom Begins: the process of personal change / Marion Pastor & Ron Luyet.
p. cm.
Includes bibliographical references
ISBN 0-914725-7902 : $11.95
1. Change (Psychology) 2. Inner Child. 3. Transactional Analysis.
4. Behavior Modification—Case studies. I. Luyet, Ron, 1945- . II. Title.
BF637.C4P38 1992
158'.1—dc20
                                              92-38395
                                              CIP

Contents

Acknowledgments

It is a privilege to be able to express our deep gratitude and appreciation to the many people who have contributed extraordinary talent, energy, and devotion to the development of the therapeutic process described in this book (most often referred to simply as "the Process"), as well as to the book itself.

We want to thank the skillful and dedicated senior teacher/ therapists at the Institute for Personal Change in San Francisco: Dorothea Hamilton, Kathy Tamm, Susan Turnwall, Steve Turnwall and James Cusack. They have been our valued colleagues and good friends for ten years and more. Each of them has made strong personal contributions to the power and effectiveness of the Process as it is taught at our Institute.

All of the teacher/therapists at the Institute, including those colleagues and friends who have worked with us more recently—Caroline Andrew, Jo Saia, Chris Jenkins and Jamie Zimron—are represented in the four teacher/therapists portrayed in the book, Dorothea, Kathy, Marion and Ron.

For the Process itself, we want to thank Robert Hoffman, who designed and originally put into practice its structure and most of its crucial individual elements. His vision and conviction brought this work into being and sustained it for many years. All of the senior teacher/therapists at the Institute owe much to our years of association with him.

We would like to acknowledge Claudio Naranjo, Ph.D., and Ernest Pecci, M.D., and the many others, such as Miriam Brandstatter, Julius Brandstatter, and Ron Kane, who were involved in the early development of the Process. We also want to thank Will Schutz for the concepts about truth, awareness and responsibility which Ron has integrated into the Process.

For their invaluable assistance in the writing of the book, we want to thank Nancy Brumbach, writing consultant, for her firm but gentle editorial hand and her gift for organization, and Steve Burton, who gave so generously of his clarity of thought, his skills in editing, and his loving encouragement. Many thanks, too, to the others who read the manuscript in its various stages and contributed editorial critiques, suggestions, proofreading, and enthusiasm: Elaine Baskin, Dennis Briskin, Nancy Carleton, Elaine Chernoff, Andrea Danzig, Karen Gulick, Elliot Gould, Dorothea Hamilton, Sheila Madden, Anita Margrill, Freda Morris, Cheryl Radetsky, Daryn Stier, Serena Stier and Kathy Tamm.

Marion especially thanks her daughter, Laana Fishman, who helped in so many caring ways, including the computer typesetting of the original manuscript, and her son, Ronn Stich Pickard, for his caring, support and wisdom.

We also want to thank Trudy Fulton-Smith, our administrative director, who not only kept the Institute running smoothly, but provided solid encouragement and support to us in getting the book done and published.

And last of all, very special and heartfelt thanks to our many graduates, whose courage and commitment, and whose passion and honesty as they speak of their personal experiences, have been an inspiration to all of us who teach this work.

Background

This book is for people who are angry at the parents who raised them badly, but who find that their anger hasn't really changed anything. It is also for people who know their parents did the best they could, but who now want to take responsibility for themselves. It is for people who have been in therapy and may have benefited a great deal, but somehow have not gotten to the root of what troubles them. It is also for people who are convinced that everything would be all right if they could just get themselves to shape up.

Many of us are aware that we react mechanically, repeating patterns we know to be destructive, living out ideas and attitudes we did not choose for ourselves. We recognize the vast distance between the self we are and the possibilities we know exist somewhere within us. This book is the story of a group of people who learned how to deal with their learned negative patterns, and thereby took a major step toward their own possibilities.

Personal notes: Marion

The human problem addressed in this book has been with me for many years. While I was still in high school, one of my teachers posed a question I'd never heard before. What would happen to children if, from the moment of birth, they could be given food and shelter and other care without any interaction with adults? I found myself arguing passionately that if children weren't exposed to all the incomprehensibly painful behavior of adults, they would grow up well and happy. The teacher assured me that I was totally wrong. She cited research showing that without their parents' caring and interactive behavior, babies do not flourish, and sometimes simply die. I had to admit that was probably true. But I knew that my conviction was also true. There is something very wrong about what most children learn from their parents.

Certainly my relationship with both of my parents was difficult. I scarcely remember my father, who disappeared from my life when I was three years old. My mother struggled hard to support my two older brothers and myself, and barely managed to keep us fed, sheltered, and clothed. This situation brought out all her emotional neediness and resentment. Furthermore, her love for us was filtered through the harsh and critical attitudes she had learned from her rigid, heavily disciplined German upbringing.

When I grew up I married a charming older man very like my father. Like my mother, after a few years, I found myself charged with the full support and care of two children—overworked, resentful, and needy. I was, however, more fortunate than my mother. When my children were in their teens, and with the encouragement and support of the man who was then my husband and is now my friend, I was able to complete a college degree in psychology and go on to graduate school in clinical social work. Later I took a teaching position at UCLA's Neuropsychiatric Institute while building a private practice in psychotherapy.

In time I found myself seriously doubtful about all the methods of therapy my colleagues and I were using: psychoanalytic, humanistic, family systems, behavior modification, gestalt, psychodrama, hypnosis, and so forth. These methods didn't seem to me to be having a profound enough effect on the people who came to us for help. Even more troublesome, my colleagues and I didn't seem to be much happier or more fulfilled than many of the people we treated. Like quite a few other people in the helping professions in the early 1970s, I left my job to explore alternative ideas about human growth and development.

Among other workshops and training programs, I took a "course" that turned out to be a brilliant innovation by Robert Hoffman, a businessman deeply interested in the human psyche. Inspired by personal discussions with psychoanalyst Siegfried Fischer, M.D., Hoffman had used both his pragmatism and his intuition to construct a new approach to personal growth. I have been involved with this approach in the various roles of student, teacher/therapist, supervisor, clinical director, and consultant for the past seventeen years.

Personal notes: Ron

My early work in psychology had little to do with the impact of childhood on our adult lives. After graduate school I worked for some years in a drug treatment center and as a community organizer in poorer communities. It was only later, when I was working for a school district doing interventions with kids in trouble, that I recognized, over and over again, how profoundly our families affect what we think of ourselves and thus how we behave and who we become.

I first heard of the Process in 1975 when it was recommended to my wife at that time by her physician because of her deep emotional pain. I was so impressed with the insights she gained and the emotional shifts she made that I signed up immediately.

I had not, from any point of view, had a "bad childhood." My twin sister and I were adopted in our first few weeks by generous, kind people. At the beginning of my Process I could not see what the difficulty in my childhood had been. But I found that there was difficulty in dealing with the unconscious images I carried of my never-known biological parents. There was difficulty in growing up with parents who were in many ways out of touch with their own wishes and desires and feelings. Though I deeply appreciate the positive gifts my adoptive parents gave me, it became clear in my Process work that having taken on their attitudes about the avoidance of conflict, of strong feelings, and of knowing what one would really want was a great disadvantage in my adult life.

With the Process my life began to make sense. The doors opened to reowning myself. I saw the powerful effect the Process had on other people, too, saw them becoming able to make decisions that changed their lives. It worked, that's what I cared about.

I have been almost continuously involved with this transformative therapy since 1975. In addition to being a teacher/therapist at our Institute, I've had the privilege and pleasure of being the chief presenter of the Process, and of leading workshops around the country. I've found that my own personal journey continues to deepen and my heart to soften in the presence of our courageous group members as they face and work through the pain of childhood and begin to find their own truth.

I have learned that we can care deeply for ourselves and through that self-care open our hearts to others who are caught in pain and suffering. We can explore with excitement the ever- evolving nature of our own being, the incredible gift of being able to discover and create the meaning of our own existence. We can take actions in the world that reflect a growing connectedness and caring for all creatures on the earth and for the earth itself. Feeling the stardust in our own being, we can open in awe to this great unfolding experiment in conscious awareness that we all share.

"The Process"

Robert Hoffman's original approach included a series of thera-peutic experiences that dealt in depth with the problem almost all of us have--the problem of being mired in the negative attitudes and behavior we learned in childhood. Despite Hoffman's unorthodox background, a number of open-minded psychiatrists, psychologists, and other health professionals became enthusiastically involved in the development of what came to be called "the Process." It was clear to us that the Process was a remarkable tool for personal growth.

The Process is different from almost all other forms of psycho-therapy in that the carefully planned, structured and time-limited series of sessions are taught like a course.

- The direct goal is to teach people to transcend the painfully limited views of themselves and the world they learned when they were children, and to free themselves from their leftover emotional dependency on their parents.
- The clearly comprehensible intellectual framework is con-firmed by the emotional experiences of the participants.
- The emotional, intellectual, and spiritual aspects of the self are temporarily separated from each other, in order to understand them and work with them powerfully and effectively.

- The immense forces of anger and forgiveness are used carefully and meaningfully.
- A remarkable level of intensity and involvement is evoked, as well as a strong coalition between teacher/therapists and the members of each group.

The Process is based on the fact that almost every one of us needs to go through essentially the same steps to break free of our negative childhood learnings. We need (1) to recognize our parents' attitudes and behavior during our childhood, (2) to realize how we have internalized their attitudes and behavior and how pervasively we are controlled by them in our adult lives, (3) to access the strength within us to break away from these adopted belief systems and patterns, and (4) to achieve integration and healing through forgiveness of both our parents and ourselves.

Powerful tools such as guided imagery, pointed inquiry, experiences of reliving and releasing the past, and new learning are used. These methods can help us see how the beliefs about ourselves and the world we acquired in our childhoods have left us functioning far below our potential, unable to really love or accept love, or to be fully effective in the world. These same methods can also help us access the wise and beautiful essential nature within each of us, and free us from the negative patterns that separate us from it.

The theory and techniques of the Process are consistent with much research and practice in psychodynamic and humanistic psychology as well as with the more recent transpersonal psychologies that call upon the wisdom of the spiritual traditions. The structure and intensity of the Process, however, appear to be unique. Its structure permits the sense of order and expectation of success with which one approaches a well-organized course in school. Its intensity carries participants far beyond their usual limitations. All of this inspires confidence and commitment in both teacher/therapists and group members.

In writing this book we wanted to share with you (to the extent that can be done through a book) the experience of going through the intensive, time-limited, carefully structured Process taught at the Institute for Personal Change in San Francisco. We made no attempt to focus on the ongoing experience of any particular group member, but rather aimed to give a cross section of the deeply felt reactions of many people going through different stages of this work.

The group followed in the coming chapters was reconstructed from several different groups at the Institute for Personal Change. Each person portrayed is an amalgam of a number of people who have taken the Process there. Their names, of course, are fictitious. The four teachers portrayed in the book are also an amalgam of the teachers at the Institute, although the real names of the authors, Marion and Ron, and those of two senior teachers, Dorothea and Kathy, are used. The written material quoted was taken from notes of our graduates, who graciously and gladly gave permission for their work to be used. The dialogue was edited from tape-recorded group sessions.

How to approach the exercises

You can find a deeper understanding of your own life and a greater opening to the freedom that can be yours through responding thoughtfully and honestly to the questions in the exercises at the end of each chapter. You can make real movement toward becoming your own person rather than the person your parents brought you up to be. You can build a profound commitment to yourself and to your own growth.

Please remember that doing these exercises on your own is not the same as doing this work in a group with the guidance of experienced teachers. The members of the group depicted in the book have strong support from the teacher/therapists who are working closely with them, and from each other. These exercises are designed, however, to give you something of the experience of doing the work of the Process as it is taught at the Institute for Personal Change.

We recommend that you do each set of exercises after you have read or reviewed the chapter they refer to. They will be easier to understand and touch you more deeply in the context of the material in that particular chapter. The material is progressive and is most valuable if each step is done in its turn, and none is skipped.

Write out your answers to the exercises in the form of an ongoing journal. (If one of your learned traits is to have difficulty with writing, you can talk your answers into a tape recorder for later listening.) It is crucial to make some kind of record for yourself, so that you can keep track of your experiences, since the effect of the work is cumulative.

Be sure to write down or tape both your *thoughts* and your *feelings* (emotional responses) in regard to the questions. One way of separating your thinking reactions from your emotional reactions is to make a line down the middle of your pages, putting your opinions and ideas about the material on one side and your feelings about it (happy, sad, angry, alone, etc.) on the other side.

If you find your mind wandering or providing you with excuses for stopping before you planned to, that is often a cue that the material you are working on may be particularly painful to you. If you allow yourself to stay with it and go through the pain, you can find a deeper level of understanding, strength, and commitment to yourself. Be sure to give yourself enough time and space afterwards to experience the feelings that may arise in you as a result of doing each of the exercises.

Do not, however, push yourself beyond what your own inner guidance tells you is right. If you find yourself becoming unduly anxious, you should stop doing the exercises, or else continue them with the help of a therapist who is familiar with the issues raised in the book.

STAGE I: AWARENESS

Chapter One: Plunging In

The work begins

The ten women and seven men meeting for the first session of the
Process hope to change their lives. They look pretty much like any
group of people dressed casually for shopping or the movies, but
there is a palpable air of nervousness and excitement among them.
In joining this group they have committed themselves to a major
investment of time, money and energy over the next three months.
All but two of them are here because of friends or relatives who
experienced fundamental change in themselves through doing this
work. Nevertheless, most of them feel uncertain that they will be able
to get what they want out of the Process. Some are worried that they
won't be able to live up to what they think is expected of them. Their
hopes are high, but they don't really know what is going to happen.

The session is held in a big, carpeted, well-lit room, decorated only
with green plants and muted draperies. The members of the group sit
facing the four teacher/therapists, Kathy, Dorothea, Marion and
Ron, who are seated at the front of the room. The classroomlike
setting is intentional, to begin rekindling childhood sensations. At
this first meeting most of the group are strangers to each other. The
teachers, though, are better informed. Each group member was
interviewed before being accepted, and asked to write an extensive
personal history.

Personal history notes

Cheryl is twenty-four years old and works as a computer programmer. She was brought up as the alternately spoiled and abused daughter of a broken marriage. In her personal history, she wrote:

> *I feel like I have been hurting for so long. I can hardly remember a time when doubts, insecurities and anger weren't a part of me. I'm scared that I'll always feel like this. It's that vague sense that other people are worthy of being loved and of loving one another, but it's not for me to experience. I hate myself right now for feeling like this. What a paradox that I hate myself for hating myself so much. It is really painful for me to see this and admit to these feelings.*

Mike is forty, a highly successful design engineer. He comes from a stable, hard working, Midwestern family. He is not the sort of person who would have started this effort on his own. His wife threatened to leave him if he didn't do something to learn to relate better to her and their two children. He wrote:

> *I don't love myself very much, don't feel lovable or valuable. I don't know myself well, I'm not sure what I like or feel. I really don't know how to have fun or relax. I have little patience for doing things with my wife and children. I'm very reluctant to participate and express myself in groups, very uncomfortable with unstructured situations, strangers, life.*

Kathleen, in her midthirties, teaches at a private school. Both her parents were alcoholic during her childhood, though her mother no longer drinks. Her mother, in fact, took the Process two years ago, and urged her to do so. Kathleen wrote:

> *I've been in three or four serious relationships, but none of them have worked out, and I get desperate about that. My life doesn't seem to be going anywhere. I know there really is a beautiful, authentic person buried somewhere in me, but I haven't been able to find her. Sometimes I start crying when there doesn't seem to be any good reason for it. I'm beginning to think maybe I'm depressed a lot.*

The group session

Ron, the teacher who leads most of the group sessions, is big and solid, with a relaxed and easy manner. At this first meeting he talks for a while about the need to recognize the tenderness and vulnerability of the child who still lives and hurts within each one of us. "The child we were has not been left behind," he tells the group. "Together with all its memories, it still exists within us." He speaks of how our perceptions of the world become distorted by ignoring that inner child's existence.

He talks about the adult intellect, full of ideas about the way things should be, and also about the beauty and reality of the spiritual nature that is part of each person. He promises that each of these aspects of them will receive full attention during the course.

He points out how hard it is to admit, sometimes even to recognize, one's own negative emotions, attitudes and behavior. But nothing can change until it has been openly acknowledged. It will become possible for the members of the group to do that as they see that they were genuinely innocent, that they learned these patterns from their parents when they were too young to choose differently.

To begin building the atmosphere of mutual trust that will permit genuine self-inquiry in the group, Ron tells them, "You are starting together on a voyage of exploration—getting to know yourself and the other people in this room in a different way than you have probably ever known anyone. We are going to ask you to introduce yourselves to each other now, but not as people usually introduce themselves. For instance, don't tell us what you do for a living, or how much education you have. Try out the idea that these aren't the most important things we need to know about you."

He asks them to stand and introduce themselves to each other only with their names and a few sentences describing the pain in their lives that brought them here. There is a long silence. Some people look startled, shift in their chairs, glance at each other or steadfastly refuse to look up for fear they will be called on.

Ann, a young woman sitting in the front row, volunteers first. She is flat-stomached, jeans riding low on her hips. She wears no makeup, and her curly brown hair is cropped close. Her manner is likeable and hesitant. "My trouble is that no matter what I do I never feel that it's really any good. I never feel satisfied. I don't need anyone else to criticize me, I can do it all myself." Her voice drops. "I'm just so angry at myself all the time." She sits down abruptly.

Kathy, another of the teachers, says simply. "Thank you, Ann. And you don't even have to tell us how much criticism you got when you were a little girl."

Ann nods somberly. "Yes, that's true. My mother and my father were always after me. Nothing I ever did was good enough for them."

Kathy adds, "And so nothing you ever do is good enough for you now, is it?"

They go on—the familiar, painful stories. Some people give earnest explanations without discernible emotional involvement. Some break into tears as they speak. Some can hardly get a few words out. Others can't stop talking. The teachers do not always draw out the connection to childhood. They know it will become more and more obvious as the work deepens.

"I'm here because I seem to have a very deep lack of self-confidence that started before I can remember. I feel a lot of guilt and a lot of fear and I'm always doing things for other people but I can't seem to take care of myself. Sometimes I feel as if I don't have a self."

"I feel separated from people and lonely."

"I'm here because I have a sense that there are some very deep bad feelings I have about myself that go back to my childhood. And I really want to get beyond them."

The group members begin to acknowledge their feelings of personal deficiency to each other in the permissive and supportive atmosphere set by the teachers. Beyond their words, though, the very way each of them stands and speaks unwittingly demonstrates what they learned about themselves from their parents (or from the other adults who functioned as substitute parents to them).

Peter looks older than his thirty years. His shoulders are rounded, and his light brown hair is already beginning to thin. He is from an intact family, his mother a community leader, his father a business-man, largely absent from the home. He says, "I get depressed and angry a lot, but I often don't let myself notice it." A rueful smile, and then a shadow of anger in his voice. "When things are going wrong, I generally don't notice that either—until something explodes in my face. And then I get so anxious it's hard for me to function."

"What kind of things have gone wrong recently?" Marion, another of the teachers, encourages him to go beyond his careful presentation.

"Well..." He hesitates, chews his lips, makes a decision, and then the words come out fast: "My wife left me for my best friend last year. And I thought everything was just great between us. Looking back, what was going on was so obvious that I don't know how I could have missed it."

Ron cuts in, "Maybe there were some things going on in your family that you weren't supposed to see when you were a child?"

Peter considers his suggestion and says slowly, "I don't know. Except maybe I wasn't supposed to see that my mother had any faults at all. She always acted as if my father was the whole problem. Up until recently, I never recognized that she was a long way from perfect, too."

"If you were supposed to be blind to what your mother was really like when you were a child, it isn't surprising that you don't notice important things today, is it?" Marion asks. Then she adds, "You know, there is a silent agreement in every family on what can and what cannot be talked about. Therapists who work with alcoholic families (and what happens in alcoholic families is only an exaggeration of what goes on in all poorly functioning families) refer to that agreement as 'don't see it, don't feel it, and don't talk about it.' Children are usually trained day by day not to see any truths that are uncomfortable for their parents to face. They learn not to admit, even to themselves, what they know."

Sitting in the front row, his somewhat prominent jaw tense, Brad speaks next. "My pain right now is thinking about my fourteen-year-old son. My God, what have I done to him?"

That gets a response from Dorothea, the fourth teacher. Dorothea has three grown children and just became a grandmother for the first time. "This is not the time to worry about your son," she says firmly. "You only acted as you were trained to do by your own parents. This is the time to think about the little boy you carry inside of you. Your relationship with your son will begin to change as you understand your own inner child better. Then you'll be able to be a real father to your son."

"Hey, wait a minute!" Elaine, a large-boned, strong-featured woman in her late forties, sounds a bit relieved and triumphant. Her cultured and affluent family had indulged in the hysterical and violent rages that punctuated her childhood only behind the closed doors of their mansion in upstate New York. "If that is true of us as parents, it's also true of our mothers and fathers! They were doing the best they could, considering what they learned from their parents!"

"So there is no point in doing this work, right?" Ron teases her gently. Most of the group have already warmed to Ron's somewhat humorous and persuasive manner. They smile with him now, recognizing in Elaine (and also in themselves) the desire for an excuse not to have to confront their own mothers and fathers.

Elaine looks puzzled, so Ron continues. "Of course, what you say is true. But has knowing that helped you?" He points out that such knowledge is only a concept to her and hasn't changed anything. They will look at their mother's and father's sides of the story after they have worked with the depth of their grief and anger about what they missed in their childhoods. If they focus on understanding their parents right now, they will only be sabotaging themselves.

"This work is done in stages," he explains. "We need to stay with the stage where we are. What would have happened to you if you had criticized one of your parents when you were a child?"

Elaine shudders involuntarily, "They would have killed me."

"See," Ron says to the class. "It takes an enormous amount of courage to do this work. Elaine isn't kidding. When she was a child she really felt that she couldn't tell the truth about the kind of parents she had or she would die. And inside she still feels that way." He looks directly at Elaine. "You won't die," he assures her. "You will begin to live when you stand up to them."

Elaine nods, but her body relaxes only a little.

Lily speaks next. She is a successful businesswoman, but tonight

6

she seems mousy and anxious. She looks down as she says softly, "I feel that I don't really have a life. I feel that everybody is running my life for me. I have lots of fear, and now I'm really afraid, standing up in front of everybody. And I just can't do anything to hurt my mother."

Marion tells Lily with gentle emphasis that none of the teachers wants her to do anything that will hurt her mother. She reminds the class that they will not be confronting their actual mothers and fathers, but the destructive images of them they carry around in their heads. She reminds them also that when the work is done they will be able to have a much more authentic and positive relationship with their actual mothers and fathers.

Mike places his writing materials neatly aside when it is his turn to speak of the pain in his life. "I've come to the conclusion that I need to get in touch better with my emotions—I live in my head too much of the time. Emotions weren't permitted when I was growing up. You were just supposed to do as you were told."

"What was permitted?" Kathy asks.

"What was permitted was getting your homework done, doing your chores, going to church, going to Sunday School, saying yes ma'am, and yes sir, and keeping your room and your fingernails clean!" Mike can actually get into grievances and resentment quite easily, though it is clear that he has little idea of the hurt or real anger that lies underneath.

Writing a description of how they experience each session is part of the assigned homework. In his notes about this first session Mike wrote:

> What first came to my mind as my answer to the question was "I'm not happy. I'm not really enjoying my life," and then I criticized myself for that answer. "Brilliant, Mike! Your main pain is that you're not happy! Profound!" But it also felt like a blinding insight.

The problem

Most of us don't have to search very far within ourselves to come upon feelings of personal deficiency, though our lives may look good

7

from the outside. Many of us suffer from anxiety, depression, or perhaps simply an ongoing sense of dissatisfaction with our lives. We may experience a lack of connectedness, an inability to love or be loved or to take genuine pleasure in what we do.

Such inner experience feels as if it occurs without our choice, automatically. We think of ourselves as being easily angered, or often depressed, or perhaps unable to respond to anything with very much enthusiasm or hope, even though we may also know there is more than that to us.

Why can't we be the person we know in our hearts we could be? One clear and workable perspective has provided an invaluable answer. We cannot be the self that is possible for us because, in our childhoods, we learned to believe that we are less than that—much less than that.

From the beginning, we attempted to become what we believed our parents wanted us to be by adopting their beliefs, attitudes and behaviors, or by trying to fulfill the open or covert admonitions they gave us. Though it was often mother's or father's fearful or resentful behavior that was adopted, the unconscious intention was always the same: "If I am like you, you will surely accept and love me."

As little children, we learned to act (and think and feel) in ways that we hoped would gain our mothers' and fathers' approval. We didn't act (or think or feel) in ways they disapproved of unless that was the only way we could get their full attention. In either case, we gave up our own selves in order to please our parents, and to avoid the pain and anxiety of real or imagined rejection. As adults, we automatically transfer this pattern to other people who are important to us.

Almost all children believe that it is their own fault if they are not loved as they want and need to be, and therefore they must somehow change themselves. It is in the attempt to become what we think our parents want that we lose our own reality and lead lives that are inauthentic. We are cut off from our true peace and joy and power.

Our negative beliefs about ourselves and the world, however, are not really connected to the parents we know as adults. Our beliefs are based on the memories we carry in our minds of the parents of our childhood (or of the other adults who functioned as substitute parents). These memories, these images, act like a pair of defective glasses that were fastened in front of our eyes when we were so young and vulnerable that we could not protest. From then on, everything we see is distorted by the flaws in our invisible glasses. But we were not born with such glasses. We came into the world fresh and new and open. We needed to be nourished in an environment of entirely reliable and consistent acceptance, love, and support to feel safe enough to flower into our true selves.

Each of us was once a newborn baby whose deepest need beyond physical necessities was simply to love and be loved unconditionally. Few children are so blessed, because few parents are able to give unconditional love. Worse, some parents are far less able than others because of their own history of having been abused as children, or because of addictions and other personal problems. And even the best intentioned parents suffer from their own anxieties, their own frustrated needs and feelings of dissatisfaction. Moreover, no matter how much parents may wish to be loving, how can they fully love and approve of their child who seems like part of them, since they do not fully love and approve of themselves?

Young children, however, can't grasp the truth that the real causes of the negative messages they receive lie within their parents. They know only that they are not being completely accepted and valued. No young child can dare to recognize that there is something wrong with the mother and father upon whom their life depends. That would make the world too unsafe.

Accepting the implications

Knowing all this doesn't necessarily help. We may be aware that many of our negative personality traits originated in childhood. We may even know that we are often mired in a destructive reenactment of our childhood relationship to our parents. But it is agonizingly difficult for most of us to accept the full implications of what it means to have been taught by our parents to react in the ways we do.

There are four main reasons for this:

First, we may be afraid to change our accustomed ways of seeking our parents' love and approval, even when those ways haven't worked. We are convinced (often unconsciously) that the only possibility of finally gaining their love is to cling to what we learned from them. At some level, most of us still believe that we must have mother's and father's approval before we can fully live—and that somehow, someplace, some day, we will finally do the right thing and we will get it.

Second, we may believe (again, usually unconsciously) that we deserve to suffer. When we were children, and didn't behave as our parents wanted us to, they usually made us feel guilty. Guilt is the belief that we have done something wrong and should be punished for it. To children, the reverse belief then comes easily: if we were suffering the punishment of not being completely loved, it must mean that we (and not they) did something wrong.

Third, the destructiveness involved in these learnings from childhood is often difficult to recognize. Along with all the ways that we were taught that we should be, we also learned that we must not question what we were being taught. The child within us still worries that such questions will bring on the very disapproval and rejection we were trying so desperately to avoid in the first place.

Fourth, we know that we would not have been born without our parents, or in most cases even survived our childhood without their care. In truth, we usually do have much reason to be grateful. Often our parents did the best they could for us, at great cost to their own energy and resources. However, most of us also have good reason to feel resentful when we look clearly at the consequences of our parent's negative attitudes and behavior on our lives (regardless of how much we may also appreciate the good things they have done for us). It is our parents who taught us to become as limited as we are, instead of the beautiful, powerful, loving beings we could be had we been given the unconditional love and acceptance we needed.

Consequently, we often find ourselves with conflicting feelings. When we try to give ourselves permission to experience and express our anger about the suffering our parents' behavior caused us, another part of us points out the reality that they were doing the best they could, given their situation. When we try to experience understanding and compassion for our parents, the grief and anger within us refuses to be ignored. We are caught in the middle—angry, but guilty for our anger—wanting to be compassionate, but full of unresolved resentment.

We can free ourselves to become what we were meant to be. First, though, we must fully acknowledge the negativities we learned from our parents, and trace how these negativities are affecting our lives now—how they prevent us from recognizing our needs and fulfilling them in ways that are authentic and positive. The early sessions are focused on this task.

The group session

With the teachers' encouragement, the members of the group continue to explore the pain in their lives. A big, suntanned young man sitting in the back of the room speaks next. "I'm angry all the time," Arnold says grimly. "I'm always getting into fights and I'm afraid I'll kill somebody one of these days." He sits back as if that completes his statement, but Kathy asks, "Who was angry in your family?"

"Nobody was angry like me. I never knew my real Dad and my stepfather always controlled himself. You could feel all this rage in him, the hard way his words would come out, the way he'd just get up and leave the room if he didn't like what was happening, the way he always said 'no,' all the time, without even stopping to talk about things—but he never raised his voice." Arnold's hands balled into fists as he continued. "But I did, I started fighting back right after my Mom married him when I was six."

Internalizing our parents

We take within ourselves the attitudes and behaviors of our parents in three major ways. One is to adopt them directly. Arnold adopted into himself his stepfather's unexpressed rage, but since his mother was often hysterically emotional, Arnold learned from her to express his anger outwardly. Like many children, he thought he had given up the attempt to be loved when he rejected his stepfather and became rebellious. His rebellion, however, was only another way of staying connected and dependent. Rebellious actions are not freely

11

chosen; they are still only a reaction to the person in authority.

The second way of reacting to our parents' attitudes and behaviors is to see them in others. If father was a liar, we think people are lying to us; if he ignored us, we expect to be ignored; if he abused us, we expect to be abused. Many of the members of the group, whose fathers had dominated and repressed them, are already afraid of Ron simply because he is an authority figure. Either adopting our parents' attitudes and behaviors into ourselves, or seeing them in others, causes great confusion in our adult relationships because our predetermined reactions are so often inappropriate to the situation at hand.

The third—and ultimately the most damaging thing we can do with a trait of our parents—is to treat ourselves the same way they treated us. We become insensitive to ourselves, or we lie to ourselves, or we ignore our own needs and abuse ourselves either physically or emotionally. Kathleen, who speaks next, has not copied her mother's addiction to alcohol so far, but she treats herself as her mother treated her when she was a child—she ignores her own needs and devalues herself.

The group session

Kathleen says, "What I'm most aware of right now is the great lengths I go to not to be aware of my feelings, not to feel any pain whatsoever, and I think in doing that I've just isolated myself from people and from myself."

Then there is Margie, a sturdy little woman, sixty-six years old, never married, a faithful worker at her church for thirty-five years before she retired. She came upon a level of anger she never dreamed existed within her in a weekend workshop she'd been persuaded to try some months earlier. Driven by this astonishing discovery, she is determined to find out more about herself before it is too late. A great deal of courage underlies her timid manner, as she begins to sort out how she has taken her parents' negativities into herself.

She speaks very softly. "I'm here because I feel burdened all the time. Even though I'm supposed to be retired, life is always work and very little joy." She takes a deep breath and plunges on in a shaky

12

voice. "I know I've been a critical and resentful person all my life, and I'm beginning to remember that my father was that way, and my mother, too. But I went to Catholic school and the nuns were awfully critical too, and I was scared of them. Maybe they were really the ones I learned it from?"

Dorothea agrees that children are often affected strongly by people other than their parents, and by inescapable events in their lives. The effects other people or happenings may have, however, largely depend on what the child learned from mother and father about his or her self-worth and lovability.

Judy rises hesitantly and a bit clumsily. She speaks in a whisper of the lack of love and closeness and connectedness in her life, and how none of her relationships ever work out. She hasn't been able to decide what career she should have and just drifts from job to job. She ends each sentence with a nervous little laugh. Then she looks at Ron to see if she said it right and abruptly sits down. She clearly expects no great respect or support from the teachers.

Living with our childhood

We all carry within us the experiences we had in childhood. Most of us, though, have learned not to hear our inner child's weeping or raging. We have learned not to listen to the messages from our inner selves. Often we don't know what we feel, or even what we really think. We still experience the world as threatening to our fragile self-esteem, just as mother and father often were threatening to us when we were children. We still feel each critical remark as a stinging attack indicating that we are not loved, and are therefore in danger. Most of us as adults are still emotionally dependent, that is, reactive and vulnerable, to our parents or to anyone in whom we see the image of our parents.

The group session

Ron reminds the class that the reason their childhood experience still matters is because it is still affecting what they do and how they feel at every moment. He spells it out concretely: "One of the main sources of information about yourself, about your history, and about

13

your future is to notice how you are responding in each moment to whatever is happening. That can be hard, because whatever you're doing is probably so familiar to you that it feels like it is you. During these thirteen weeks we want you to assume that the anxiety and distrust, the hostility, the desire to please at any cost, or the numbness you may notice in yourself is not you; it's simply the way you were trained to think and feel and behave when you were a child. It was brainwashed into you a long time ago."

The teachers will often come back to this theme both in individual sessions and in the group meetings. They will say over and over again in many ways, "You are worth knowing, and the way to learn to know yourself is to pay attention to yourself as we do this work. The programs you learned as a child are not your real self. You can learn to tell the difference."

Ron continues, "You'll be working with us in the Process only for the next three months, but we hope you will be learning about yourself for the rest of your life. The path we're on is not to get to a place called 'cured.' It's more like a path that will lead you deeper and deeper into a sense of who you are, what you want for yourself, and what adds meaning to your life. You are here to clear away the roadblocks in your path, and to learn the tools for keeping it clear."

He goes on to point out that much of the work they will be doing is intended to bring their unconscious experience to a conscious level. One of the most useful aids in this task, he tells them, will be to notice what happens when they approach something that triggers their anxiety. When doing the homework makes them anxious, for instance, they may find themselves thinking, "If I say what I really think, my teacher might get mad at me, or she'll think I'm dumb." Noticing that fear is a step toward freedom. Going ahead and writing it anyway is an even more crucial step. "One thread to hold on to as you go through this work," Ron says, "is to try your best to keep telling the truth. This is an ability most of us have lost. We often don't know what's true for us, and when we do we are scared to death to say it." He adds that this didn't just happen by itself. Because most of us were disapproved of when we told the truth about how we experienced things as we were growing up, we learned to avoid the truth and to lie.

"The trouble is, it's very hard and wearing to keep having to tell lies," he continues. "You may not even notice when you are lying. But when you do you won't like yourself very well at the end of the day, or know yourself very well. And no one else can know you, either. I'd like you to experiment with telling the truth more and more, at least during these thirteen weeks, and just see what that feels like."

Arnold blurts out, "But you can really get yourself in trouble telling the truth. You tell your boss you think he's a jerk and see what it gets you. Fired!"

Ron grins and nods. "Probably would." Then he is very serious. "The trouble is that usually when we tell people the truth about what we think of them, we don't tell the whole truth, we stop at the first level. We don't usually tell them what they've done to make us think that, or how it made us feel when they did it, or what we think it means when they do that, or what it makes us feel about ourselves. And we very seldom tell them how we learned as children to feel so outraged when somebody acts like that. Telling the truth has a lot of levels."

Arnold looks baffled. "I don't get it. What do you mean?"

"Well," Ron suggested, "suppose you told your boss that when he yelled at you in a meeting it made you angry and afraid, because you thought it meant that he wasn't paying attention to all the stuff you do well, and that he might fire you. And then, what if you went even deeper and admitted that sparked a lot of your uncertainties about your own competence. And then you went still deeper and added that you felt unsure of yourself around him because your father never seemed to think you had any value at all."

"Tell my boss all that!" Arnold demands, as if thunderstruck. The group roars.

Ron laughs with them. "No. Not until you are ready, and maybe not in all situations even then. Though it is my own conviction that the more you tell the truth the simpler your life gets. I am suggesting that you begin practicing telling the truth in here where it is safe and where you can get some clear feedback on what you are doing.

"All the things we are doing here will work better if we keep committing ourselves to tell the truth about what's going on in the sessions and in our lives. In a way the whole Process is about coming to our own truth and finally feeling comfortable with it. When we tell ourselves the truth about the difficult stuff inside us we can work with it, and then we are more able to tell other people the truth about us."

Written homework

The members are given instructions for written homework that will take them at least eight hours to complete before the next weekly session. Part of their homework is to give their understanding of what went on in the session and also their emotional responses to it. Writing it down will clarify it for them, and deepen their experience. It will also permit their own individual teacher to know in detail what they are experiencing, and to tell what kind of help they may need. The rest of the homework expands on what is done in the session.

For instance, they are given a long and comprehensive list of negative behaviors, attitudes and feelings (such as hostile, stingy, intolerant, withdrawn, dependent, and so on) and asked to identify all those their parents exhibited while they were growing up. This list is part of the total emphasis during these first weeks on recognizing the negativities that were modeled for them when they were children—the negativities that are still running their lives.

In his homework Mike automatically used his father's critical stance in handling his anxiety about the first session. He wrote:

> *It was almost fifteen minutes past the hour by the time we got started, and I was very conscious of that. I usually think of myself as open-minded and tolerant, but I am critical and intolerant and unforgiving about people wasting my time. I felt disgusted and angry and impatient. I told myself, "If these people cared about what they were doing and cared about me, they wouldn't waste my time like this."*

His notes after the group were able to share the pain in their lives with each other, though still reserved, have a different tone.

> *I did feel touched at times, and quite a bit of what people said struck home. I'm beginning to feel that I'm in the right place,*

16

and that I do want to do this work. I guess there are a lot of things going on in my life I've never been willing to look at very hard.

Judy was more directly in touch with her anxiety. She wrote:

My reaction to the group at first was a lot of fear. I was scared of being with the other students, their new faces, and the new teachers. I was scared of my own emotions. What will you find out about me, what will I find out about myself? I felt like crying and I am not really sure why. I was uncomfortable sitting in the chair. I wished I was home.

When people started talking about their pain, I was surprised to see that so many people who looked so together felt that badly about themselves. It made me feel safer, like maybe it would be all right to talk about the hurtful things that happened in my childhood in front of them, after all. I'm not sure yet, though. Some of them still scare me.

17

Chapter One Exercises

Ask yourself these questions and note the answers in your journal or put them on tape.

Exercise 1

   a. Why are you reading this book (other than because of a recommendation)? What do you hope to gain?

   b. Think about the different parts of your current life (how you relate to people important to you, what your work life is like, what you do for enjoyment, your sexuality). What is most painful to you about all that?

   c. Does thinking about what is painful in your life make you feel angry, sad, fearful, withdrawn and numb, or some other way or combination of ways?

   d. How does your purpose in reading this book relate to what is most painful in your life?

Exercise 2

   a. Sit quietly with your eyes either closed or open, whichever is most comfortable for you. Remember yourself when you were about six years old (a photo may help). Imagine returning to your childhood home at that time. Was it a house or an apartment? How many rooms were there? Imagine going inside and seeing your family sitting at the table together. What is your mother like? What happens in your relationship with her? What is your father like and what happens in your relationship with him? How do they treat you and any siblings you may have? Try other ages in your childhood, two, four, eight, ten, twelve.

     If your memories are not clear, it can be useful to talk with siblings, other relatives, or old family friends (those whom you feel can be fairly objective), to get their perspective of what your home and your parents were like when you were a child.

   b. List three of the negative traits that troubled you most about each of your parents and/or parent substitutes, for instance; controlling, cold, smothering, angry, always worried, never believed me, etc.

18

c. Looking back at your answers to Exercise 1b, can you see connections between what pains you most in your life today and the most troublesome negative traits of your parents?

Exercise 3

On a scale of 0 to 10 (0 meaning "not at all," 10 meaning "more than anything else in the world") how much do you want to be free of your negative childhood learnings, so that you can become the person you were meant to be?

Chapter Two: Emotional Child, Intellectual Adult, Spirit

Learning from visualizations

Guided imagery is one of the most effective tools we can use in exploring our inner worlds. The pictures we see in our minds can be windows into realms within ourselves we were aware of only dimly—or perhaps not aware of at all. They can help us understand what happened to us in the past, what our lives are like now, and what we can do to bring about the changes we want. We can learn to recognize and work powerfully with what we consider to be our weaknesses, and also with our strength and love and wisdom. Imagery is more than a means of inner exploration, it is also a means of self-transformation.

Using imagery to know our different selves

We can learn to use our imagery to separate out the different aspects of ourselves and make them distinct in our minds. We can see the emotional self as the child it is (few of us have grown much emotionally since childhood); the intellectual self as the adult it tries to be, and sometimes is; and the spirit within us as the luminous source of wisdom and light it truly is. The emotional child who still lives within us and our adult intellect—who is in many ways only an extension of the emotional child—have both been programmed by our early experiences. Our spiritual nature can never be programmed, and is real from the beginning. Temporarily separated in this way, they can each speak for themselves and to each other.

If you wish, you can experience these aspects of yourself through this method. Before beginning it is best to relax as much as possible, perhaps simply attending to your breathing for a while, and letting your body get heavy. Then follow the instructions with closed eyes, either taping them first or having someone read them to you.

Bring to your mind a beautiful, serene outdoor scene, with the kind of trees and flowers, meadows and mountains, water and sky that you like best. It can be someplace you've been before, or someplace entirely new that appears to you in the moment. Spend a few moments appreciating this place and feeling its peace and welcome. Feel the warm, gentle sun and a soft little breeze on your face and body. Listen to the music of the water, and maybe the songs of birds, or the leaves rustling. This is an inner sanctuary you have summoned into existence, to which you can return any time you want.

Now bring in an image of yourself at about the age of four or five. Some people remember clearly how they looked, others find themselves having to remember a photograph. Don't be concerned if the image is not distinct. Seeing images clearly is like musical ability; some people are naturally talented, and some only minimally, but everyone can enjoy music. The vividness of your images has nothing to do with their effectiveness.

Let the child in your image move from inside of you to a position a few feet away, facing you. Notice how your child is dressed, and sits or stands, and seems to be feeling. Ask if your child is willing to talk to you and what he or she wants to tell you. Do whatever helps you to get comfortable with the notion of being able to see and speak with your own inner child. Let yourself realize that most of your emotional life is carried by this inner child. Accept whatever the child says or does as a way of getting to know yourself better.

Now let an image of your intellectual adult self form. Your intellectual adult may look just like you, although such images often seem more businesslike than we usually think of ourselves. Notice his or her clothes and posture and general attitude. Sometimes the image is totally different from what we expect. One man found to his astonishment that he envisioned his intellect with multiple eyes like

22

an insect, eyes that kept peering in all directions at once, looking for danger.

Let this image of your intellect now also stand a few feet away from you, and move and speak. Ask what he or she thinks about this imagery experience you are engaged in. Again, accept what you get—this time as your intellect's opinion (and you're likely to find that he or she has a lot of opinions). Your intellect may insist that this experiment with imagery is silly. Intellects are sometimes like that.

Now with your emotional child and your intellectual adult both imaged as being outside of you and a few feet away, let yourself settle back and relax still more deeply. Remember the natural beauty of your sanctuary and look around. Now let yourself see, in the sky, but close to the horizon, a radiant, glowing ball of light. The ball of light is drifting toward you in a flowing motion that fascinates you and holds your attention. As it comes nearer, you see that in its center is a being whose peacefulness, wisdom, and strength is clearly apparent to you. The ball of light comes to rest in front of you. Someone steps out.

Notice how this person is dressed, the age, the appearance of the body and hair and face. Notice most of all the radiant love for you that glows in the eyes as they look into yours. This is your own personification of the peace, assurance, gratitude, and love of the universe.

At this point, you may recognize this entity as being part of yourself. You may know that he or she is the aspect of you that is neither emotional child nor intellectual adult, but your essential, spiritual self. On the other hand—especially if this being is a man, if you are a woman, or a woman, if you are a man—he or she may enter your life as your guide, loving friend, and wise counselor. In either case, this guiding spirit is totally beneficent and intends only the best for you.

Now turn back to your child and intellect and find out what your intellect thinks about your child. This may be something of a shock. Your intellect probably treats your child much as you were treated as a child. If there was harshness and criticism in your childhood, it is most likely still there, carried by your intellect. If you were put down, or ignored, or spoiled—all of that will almost always still exist in your intellect's attitude toward your own inner child.

Now ask your child how he or she feels about the way your intellect is behaving, and listen carefully. Often the emotional child within is hurt and angry and afraid—perhaps too afraid to speak frankly without encouragement. Sometimes hidden feelings come out in a rush, and you can learn a lot about yourself in a single sitting. Sometimes, neither the child nor the intellect is so open, and then the lesson is that they both feel very unsafe in expressing themselves. Your imagery is reflecting that. The experience will deepen with practice and patience.

Now let yourself feel the compassion your guiding spirit has for both your child and intellect and how stuck they are in automatic, programmed reactions. Feel also your spirit's recognition of their potential for being real and authentic. From the stand point of your guiding spirit, look at the interaction between your child and your intellect. See the wise and loving way your spirit relates to both of them. When you are ready to end the experience, let your spirit reach out and integrate the separate parts of you back into one. (Physically open your arms and image yourself gathering your child and intellect back into your body.)

Being programmed and being real

When we are run by our childhood programming, we automatically obey the internalized voices from our past that tell us how we are supposed to feel and conduct ourselves. These voices often are so strong and persistent that we are unable to attend to what is happening in the present. As a result, we are alienated not only from others, but from ourselves as well.

When we are real and authentic, we respond fully to the present moment. We manifest awareness, responsibility, and choice. We are spontaneous, creative, loving, powerful, and growing. We may at times be angry or sad or feel helpless, but it will be because we are responding appropriately to what is actually going on. We can permit unpleasant emotions to move through us and change, as it is natural for emotions to do.

As adults, we still carry within us a wounded child. Part of the work of personal change is to explore that wound and heal that child. Sometimes that exploration hurts. It is difficult to let ourselves feel again the helplessness, the agony, and the anger that we struggled with as children. It is even more difficult to admit that these feelings are still going on within us. The emotional child is still very young, wanting desperately to be loved, and often scared and angry and acting out.

The adult intellect likes to think it is in control of our lives, but the truth is that the emotional child within us can take over whenever the old painful feelings are touched. That's when we say things like, "I really want to clean the house today. Too bad I've got such a headache that I can't."

The emotional child

The emotional child within us is innocent. We learned the behaviors that cause us so much trouble in order to survive. We knew from the way our parents related to us that what we were simply wasn't good enough. Though they may have thought they loved us, we could tell from their attitudes and behavior that they wanted and expected us to be different. We were not acceptable as we were. So we tried to become like them, or like what we thought they wanted us to be. The child within us continues this attempt long after we are grown, whether our parents are still living or not.

Imaging and then letting our own programmed emotional child (at about the age of four or five) speak through us can give us knowledge of this part of ourselves. It can also help us recognize how much fear and reluctance we feel about delving into our childhood pain. We also can find out how much distrust we have in ourselves and those who are attempting to help us, as well as anxiety about the whole business of changing. Until we know the existence and strength of these feelings they cannot change.

When the emotional child within us is free of its programming, it feels authentic and appropriate emotions. It is spontaneous, playful, creative, and joyful. A big part of the work of personal change is to help the child within clear out the old rage and pain and longing, so that we may become the warm, exciting, rich, flowing beings that we were meant to be.

An individual session

The members of the group each do this imagery in one of their weekly individual sessions with the teacher/therapist assigned to them. Alicia's teacher is Marion. Alicia is a sociologist with two books on women's issues to her credit. Her strikingly beautiful face is framed by smooth dark hair; the heavy curves of her body are both obscured and emphasized by a loose and colorful dress. She has a delightful social manner, two litigious divorces, a son who is in serious trouble at school, and a history of battling with male superiors at work that has cost her dearly in her career. In her individual session, Alicia easily forms an image of her programmed child.

Her notes afterwards suggested a sense of wonder:

> *My child is a cute little girl with ponytails, a tooth missing, freckles on her nose, a little plump. She smiles and has mischievous eyes. She is dressed in a pinafore. When she is given a chance to speak for herself, she says about my intellect, "She knows I'm not so good, she tells me all the time. I'm lazy, and I don't like to work." The child initially resists the idea of having to do the work that we are doing and wants intellect to do it for her.*
>
> *When Marion suggests that maybe she is afraid of Mommy and Daddy, my child denies it and says, "I could kick, scream, yell, and hurt them." But then I feel a constriction in my chest which I've come to recognize as an anxiety signal. My child remembers that her parents are big and she is little. "I love them and I want them to love me. I'm afraid if I let my bad self out, I'll hurt them, kill them, and then what will happen to me?" I'm fascinated at how real the child is. That last line is so strikingly authentic to me. She knows that what really worries her is what will happen to her if her rage were let loose and destroyed her parents. As I write this I feel my stomach tensing up like a tight fist. It is not only the anger I'm afraid of, but the consequences to me of its release.*

26

The intellectual adult

The programmed adult intellect within us spends most of its time judging and criticizing us as well as everyone else, and trying to figure out how to be safe in a world it perceives as mostly hostile. It is often rigid and controlling, and likes to believe that it is in charge of our lives. It also tends to run a critical commentary about everything. "I don't like this." "That doesn't make sense." "See, that proves they don't like you." "My God, you are stupid! How could you do a thing like that?" And on and on and on.

The programmed adult intellect, however, really can't handle our lives very well. If it could, all of us would be in fine shape by now. Most of us have spent a lot of time trying to think our way out of our problems.

When the adult intellect in us is free of its programming, however, it is intelligent, perceptive and knowledgable. It is able to learn, understand, plan, and make sound decisions. It can become a valuable ally to both the emotional child and the guiding spirit.

As Alicia identifies with her adult intellect and speaks for it, she can see her strong need to be the one who is "right," and also her harshness toward the emotional child part of herself.

In her notes about the session, she wrote:

My intellect was very prim in her gray suit and sensible shoes. She seemed judgmental and self-righteous and terribly constricted. I was very surprised at how uptight and rather unhappy she is, and how unfriendly to my child. I'm really glad my intellect expressed some resistance and skepticism to begin with, though. One of my problems is always being accommodating and always being a good girl. I know what my teacher wants of me, so it is important to keep testing my sincerity. I don't want to just give a performance. I've been doing that all my life.

Our bodies

In addition to our emotional child and intellectual adult, our bodies, too, carry old stories, old information. They hold the trauma of childhood pain. Did you ever watch a child being yelled at by its mother or father? You can literally see the small body shrink into itself. If we pay attention to our body's customary ways of reacting, of carrying the weight of the world, or of trying to make itself small so it won't be noticed, we can see the truth of what happened to us in childhood. The way we hold ourselves and the contractions in our muscles are still with us as adults, even when we aren't aware of the connection to childhood experiences.

The body is the source of energy, good feelings, instinctive wisdom and grounding. Like our real intelligence and real emotions, the body begins to manifest its true possibilities as we learn to separate ourselves from our programming and come into harmony with our essential natures.

The guiding spirit

This programming of emotions, intellect, and body, however, is not the whole truth about ourselves—and somewhere inside us we all know that. All of us have had moments when we had a sense of having gone beyond what we ordinarily know of ourselves and the world. It may have been through listening to music, seeing a magnificent sunset, holding a newborn baby, knowing our lives were really in danger, or perhaps while making love. It may have been through some form of meditation or other personal growth experience.

All of us have had times when we experienced greater self-acceptance and a higher quality of life, moments when we knew that we were capable of being more loving, more effective, and far happier than we usually are. Our spiritual or essential nature (the light and truth within us) cannot be programmed. That's where our potential for real wisdom, peace, compassion, and love lies, regardless of what kinds of experiences we've had. It is our spiritual nature that makes true change possible.

It's hard to talk about our essential natures, because the experience is not really translatable into words. The Process, however, is based on the belief that all psychological and spiritual difficulties from which human beings suffer are a result of our having become separated from our own essential, spiritual natures. If that aspect of us had been acknowledged, honored, and mirrored back to us when we were children, we would know it as the core of our lives. Since it wasn't acknowledged, we are unsure in our contact with it. Some of us even think we are only our bodies, emotions, and intellects, and that's all there is to us.

Coming to know this part of themselves through guided imagery, some people experience their spiritual natures as one of their three selves. For others, this spirit seems more like a guide, an entity other than themselves, sent to help and support them.

Alicia readily contacts an image of her spiritual nature, who would help her in the difficult work to come. Later she wrote:

> *My spirit is a peaceful, glowing being in diaphanous robes with a radiant golden aura. I was really pleased to have this being with me. She took my child on her lap and said, "You will not have to grow up this time until you are ready; I will take care of you till then." I think of how my child had to be a big girl much too soon. (The same thing happened to my daughter.) I wish I had had my spirit for a mother. Then I'd have grown from the center out, rather than developing a shell and now trying to fill it up properly.*
>
> *It was great, though, when my spirit reached out and touched my intellect and told her to loosen up and my intellect did feel better and looser. But I don't think she's quite ready to give over the reins entirely just yet.*

The value of the guiding spirit

This image of our guiding spirit is not, of course, the whole of our true spiritual or essential core—for much of that level of ourselves is beyond words or images. It is rather a way of getting in touch with the qualities of our essential core, qualities such as peace, strength, compassion, wisdom, and love. Our guiding spirit is like an emissary from that level, an intermediary between the true wisdom and love of the universe and the way in which that wisdom and love is available to us as individuals. It is an expression of our contact with the deepest truth within us.

Through imagery, the members of the group are able to contact a beautiful, peaceful, powerful, and loving being in the dialogue between their different aspects—a being who already loves and accepts them and intends only the best for them. The recognition of this being makes it possible to address the work of confronting a painful childhood with hope, no matter how much despair the emotional child or the intellectual adult may feel.

Angie's experience

Angie, whose life with her schizophrenic mother and alcoholic father had been its own kind of hell, wrote in her notes to Dorothea, her individual teacher:

> *As my child, I feel sick and poisoned inside my soul; tears aren't enough. Even seeing blood on my hands would not be enough. I feel like screaming and writhing when I think of my childhood. As my intellect, I would rather that the child inside me be dead, and the memory of her and all the incidents about her be completely forgotten. That child sabotages me. I often find myself doing stupid, mean things to people, especially those closest to me. I am afraid that my emotional child will always be angry, unrelenting, violent, revengeful, paranoid.*
>
> *But then, as I imaged being my spirit, and telling my child that I would take care of her, and that she was not going to have to die, the child's tears felt like the poison was beginning to seep out of my being. As my spirit, I felt almost like I felt the night that Walter died. [Walter was an old friend whose serene and accepting death she and other of his friends had witnessed together.] I felt like there really was a part of me that had this deep sense of knowing, and a sort of joyful surrender.*

Imagery can be trusted

Some people object initially that they cannot visualize, don't usually make mental images, and would be much more comfortable sticking to words. Material is always available, however, if we stay open to what comes and don't block it out. The more we simply accept what we get, the more easily and effectively imagery works.

It is true that our usual way of communicating, not only with each other but with ourselves, is in words. We explain, describe, persuade, manipulate, and put labels on things and people with words. The difficulty is that from the first meaningful sounds we learned to make, our words have been subject to our parents' control.

They approved of us at first for making recognizable sounds at all, and we learned very early to connect the kind of feedback we were getting with the sounds we made. We learned the correct names and the correct pronunciations in the language and accent that was used in our home. At the same time, we learned that some thoughts were approved of highly, and others drew disapproval when we put them into words. Some of us were delighted to learn that certain words could upset our parents, and we used these words to force them to pay attention to us.

We learned to monitor what we said according to our expectation of the reactions we would get. This meant, of course, that our parents were the ones who really controlled our words. From the place where our parents' images reside in our minds, they still do. We often cannot communicate simply and clearly even with ourselves, because our words have not been ours from the beginning.

Imagery, though, is a way to communicate with ourselves that is not subject to control based on expected reactions. No one can tell what our inner pictures and sensations are, unless we describe them. Our image-making abilities have been subject to much less interference and much less programming than our speech. Because of this, our images can bring to our conscious minds information from within ourselves that ordinarily might never reach us. The use of imagery is a vital, available connection between our inner selves and our conscious minds. In coming to know the different aspects of ourselves through imagery, we can discover just what kind of inner struggle we are engaged in, and take a big step in the direction of the essential commitment that is necessary to create change. Our emotional, intellectual, and spiritual aspects become real to us, and a genuine alliance among them becomes possible.

Tom's experience

Tom's self-hatred is so intense that Kathy, the teacher who works with him individually, takes him back into his childhood to remind him why his emotional child is so miserable. Later he wrote:

Kathy had me be myself at about age six and visualize some of the interactions between myself and the two sets of parents I had. I found myself overwhelmed with confusion, guilt and beneath the guilt, grief. I felt terribly lonely, but I was more afraid to be with my mother, my father, and my stepmother than to be by myself. They all treated me as if I caused them trouble just by existing.

When I relived going to visit my mother, just being around her coldness and bleakness and despair, and then being told by my stepfather how much pain she was in because I didn't love her, I could feel the tightness in my belly coming up into my chest and throat.

When I got home, I was grilled by my father about every detail of my visit, and he would rant and rave at me about what a bad person my mother was and how lucky I was to have my stepmother. But he never would see that I was terrified of my stepmother's criticism and disapproval of me. I cried myself to sleep, alone in my room, almost every night during my childhood.

By now, my chest and throat were aching. Kathy asked me to see this little boy through the eyes of my adult intellect, and to say what I thought about him. I said to him, "No wonder nobody likes you; you're nothing but a pathetic little wimp." I saw him as an insecure, gangly, scared kid who couldn't do anything right.

Then she asked me to look at him through the eyes of my spirit. Suddenly I could see that he was just a little kid totally alone in an adult world that had no place for him. I gently picked up this poor scared little boy and held him close to me. I could feel his body soften, and he started to sob, his head buried safely in my chest. There was no anger in him, no resentment, only a deep longing to belong somewhere.

As my spirit, I looked deeply into his eyes and I told him that the time for being alone was over. I felt strong saying it because I knew that it was true. This boy will feel my love for him from now on.

As my spirit, I then turned to my intellect, standing next to me. I told him sternly that his reign was over. Looking deeply into his eyes, I explained that his intelligence now was to be used for the sole purpose of healing this child, and he understood. The whole thing felt very clean. No anger or hate, only determination and commitment. As my spirit, I explained to the intellect, "It is the child's turn now. You and I and Kathy and this whole Process are here for that little boy. When he is whole, you will be whole, too."

As I sat there visualizing all this, tears came to my eyes. I felt the ache in my heart releasing through the realization that my time in hell is near an end. I have never been able to cry out loud before in the presence of another person, but I did then. Kathy held me and I felt no shame, only a deep sadness that the tragedy has gone on for so long.

Though some people in the class have more difficulty than others in learning to image and identify with their different aspects, each one of them gains greater insight and begins to experience new openings into themselves. Temporary separation of these aspects of the self is a major step toward real integration.

Chapter Two Exercises

Exercise I

The visualization for this exercise is given beginning on the second page of Chapter Two. You may want to put it on tape for yourself or have a friend read it to you slowly, to give you time to follow the steps.

Begin by sitting or lying down comfortably where you will not be disturbed. Take time to relax yourself before beginning. It usually helps to close your eyes. Breathe deeply and quietly for a moment or two, paying attention to the movement of your breath. Let your thoughts quiet down. Don't be concerned about the clarity of your visualizations (some people see pictures clearly in their minds, some don't), so long as you have a sense of what is happening. As your imagery arises, be sure not to judge or censor what comes up, or to manufacture how you'd like the scene to be. Just accept what comes.

After doing the visualization, ask yourself these questions and note the answers in your journal or put them on tape.

a. Describe the appearance and attitude of your emotional child, your intellectual adult, and your guiding spirit. Describe the interaction between them.

b. Whenever there is a major decision to be made in your life, does your inner child (your emotional self) get to make the decision on the basis of what he or she wants at the moment? Or does your intellect alone make your decisions, without paying attention to the needs of your child?

c. What is it like for you to recognize the wise counsel of your guiding spirit?

d. Pick something that is an ongoing problem in your life and let your child, your intellect and your guiding spirit talk about it together, as they did in the visualization.

Remember, throughout your work with this book, separating out your inner child (in order to understand and respond to your feelings), your intellect (to be sure he

*or she is being appropriately active, but not trying to run
the whole show), and your guiding spirit (for support and
wisdom and guidance), helps at every step.*

Chapter Three: Connecting the Past to the Present

Getting feedback

The passage to freedom from being painfully mired in our childhood programming is not easy. We must go back and forth between experiencing the limitations of childhood (so that we know what they are) and learning what freedom is like (so that we know what is possible for us). Working with the emotional child, the intellectual adult, and the guiding spirit through imagery can make both the limitations and the possibilities unequivocally real. The teachers also help clarify the connections between childhood patterns and present behavior and attitudes by pointing out how both are reflected in the group members' written homework.

Before the beginning of the second session, each member of the group receives a tape from his or her teacher with clear and explicit feedback on what their homework revealed about them in the first week, and how it connects to what they learned in their childhoods. This honest commentary is sometimes hard for the members to accept, though the tapes also strongly affirm each person's essential beauty, strength and potential for change. For most, however, the fear of being seen as wrong and bad is ever present at this early stage of the work.

Before they listen to their tapes, Ron reminds them, "Remember, you can choose to treat everything you hear on your tape as evidence that something is wrong with you, or as information that will free you. If you treat it as evidence against you, you'll think, 'Oh, God, I thought I was bad. Now after this first week I know I'm shit. Look at what they told me about myself.' If you treat it as information that can free you, you'll think, 'Isn't this interesting. Look at what my teacher is pointing out about me. I recognize that. Now how did I learn it?'

"You'll find that some of the stuff we are working with is painful," Ron continued. "We are taking you into it not because we want to be mean to you, but because sometimes the only way to heal a wound is to go into it and clean it out. In spite of what it may look like to you initially, we are not being judgmental or critical of you. But when we see how you are hurting yourself, and how you are blinding yourself, we will tell you so. The amount you let it in is up to you, but we will do our best to give you the information you need to work with."

Though his message is clearly in earnest, Ron's casual delivery helps lower the anxiety in the room. The tense faces and cramped muscles begin to relax a little. He goes on to say that he knows from his own experience how strong the tendency is to punish ourselves with disapproval and self-hatred when we learn something new about ourselves. Like the other teachers, he had done this work himself. "It's the surest way to keep yourself unaware of what you are doing," he adds. "If you beat yourself up every time you become aware of something, why would you want to be aware?"

Taking responsibility

Strangely enough, while experiencing how stuck we are in our programming is hard, experiencing the possibility of freedom can also be difficult. Freedom entails responsibility, and the idea of responsibility is fearfully encumbered for most of us. In most families, "taking responsibility" for anything means to be guilty and at fault. Few parents demonstrate by their behavior that taking responsibility for oneself and for one's experience of the world is a fine and empowering way to live.

Most of us were taught that punishment for doing anything wrong is normal, and even good for us. When we lost or broke something as children, or made some other kind of mistake, we were usually punished if we were caught. And most of us learned that pattern so well that we still treat ourselves the same way. When we catch ourselves doing something we'd like to do differently, we attack ourselves.

As a result, when we are given feedback about what we say and do, we usually automatically begin to defend ourselves against what feels like an accusation. Looming above us we see our parents, who will now assess blame, fault, sin. Much as we may know that we need to explore the attitudes and behavior that result in our unhappiness and ineffectiveness, the child inside us is afraid of being declared guilty.

Feedback is sometimes painful

Some members of the group, therefore, hear any kind of feedback as a personal attack. Elaine's parents had been domineering, abusive, and rejecting of her all through her childhood. In her notes about her tape from her teacher she wrote:

> *You pointed out that I was being very judgmental of other members of the class, and I feel that you set me up. I was told to be acutely aware of my reactions and to write them down. I feel like you put me in a double bind by asking me to be open and then criticizing me for what I say. If I may say so, I think that was very poor technique on your part, because I don't feel very safe with you anymore.*

Even though Elaine is attempting to see her situation clearly, she feels so much fear, resentment, and worry about being blamed that she simply is not capable of putting aside the idea of blame. Her immediate reaction is to defend herself by turning and blaming her teacher. She needs to discover that the deeply ingrained belief that someone has to be at fault must be turned on the original source of her fear of being blamed—not in the half-convinced, fearful way such ideas were expressed in her childhood ("You're a bad mommy!"), but with full recognition of the ways in which they were bad parents indeed. It is only as she permits herself to accept that as sober truth— and to see the results of the bad parenting she received in all their painful detail—that she is willing to take responsibility for her present attitudes and behavior.

With Marion's support in recognizing how she had learned to be so harshly critical of others, and in seeing that it really was not her fault, Elaine permits herself to get a clearer picture of what is going on:

> *My parents could not take any criticism. The implication was always that I was the jerk for being so negative and ungrateful. They never listened thoughtfully and openly to complaints—rejection, denial, and defense were their automatic reactions. They probably never had the experience of criticism being offered out of love and concern for someone else's growth, so they equated criticism with hatred and condemnation. I can see myself doing the same thing.*

As she looks at her present behavior from the perspective of how she learned it from her parents, she is able to see and admit things that she kept carefully hidden all her life, even from herself. Since we can't change what we can't see, this lowering of defensiveness is essential. Elaine's notes continued:

> *I felt this tremendous sense of relief, of some sort of validation that I am not responsible for being so messed up, that my depression (which I have been very aware of for a long time) is not just fabricated or because I am crazy. It's like there is some kind of diagnosis now and I get that there are some pretty good reasons why my life has been so miserable, that I have not had much control over and am not responsible for creating. It really hurt to hear how I am, but the comments were reasonable ones, and I just wanted to cry out that I would like another chance and don't really want to be this way.*

Many of the ways in which we recreate our childhood relationship to our parents—a relationship of helpless and vulnerable children attempting to gain desperately needed love and acceptance—are so disguised that we don't recognize them. As adults, we continue to defend ourselves against what we see as criticism and invalidation in the same ways we did as children. We spend our whole lives trapped in the old and still unproductive cycle of seeking approval from others and reacting with pain and anger when we don't get it.

Appeasers, hostiles and withholders

There are three primary ways in which we defend ourselves from what we experience as rejection or punishment: we seek to appease or please, we become hostile, or we withhold and deaden ourselves. We learned to use these methods when we experienced ourselves as being attacked by our parents when we were children.

Appeasing or pleasing means that our actions are based on an attempt to buy the love of the one on whom we depend. We become hostile and rebellious when we learn that attempting to please still doesn't get us what we need. Withholding and deadening ourselves means we have cut off the vital emotional and energetic flow that should fuel our lives.

The value of these three ways of describing our attitudes and behavior lies in the fact that they are both basic and clearly recognizable. Most of us usually react to pressure in one, or possibly two, of these ways, though we are capable of all three. The members of the group were given a brief experience of guided imagery to acquaint them with their own customary behavior.

"Take a moment to relax," they are told, "and then imagine that you are in your favorite supermarket, pushing a heavily loaded cart around a corner. Another cart collides with yours, spilling many items on the floor. Notice your first reaction." Some people see themselves apologizing profusely and helping pick up the other person's things, others see themselves becoming angry and blaming, while still others see themselves retrieving their things while ignoring the other person as much as possible. Each one of these responses was learned when we were children and can be traced back to an easily angered parent, a love-buying parent, or a parent who usually ignored us emotionally. Each is an unconscious way of remaining connected to our parents by acting out the programming we learned from them. Even rebelling against our parents means that we are still reacting to them, though now with the hopeless inner conviction that now they will never love us, since we have rejected them. Many variations are possible, of course. For instance, the pattern of defending ourselves by withholding and going numb can be a reaction to a mother whose attentions and demands were overwhelming. But even then we learned that way of coping with her from someone, perhaps from a withdrawn father.

Elaine's notes show that her primary response under pressure is hostility. Cheryl's main need is to please everyone. In response to her first tape, she tried to agree enthusiastically with what her teacher said, and at the same moment to appease her parents.

It felt wonderful to realize that anyone was reading what I wrote so carefully, and I want to thank you for all your time and attention. You were absolutely right; my mother was angry a great deal of the time and she did hit me a lot, and I can see where I have contradicted myself in how I describe her. I can see how I experienced one thing in my life and I have told you a story about it which sounds different. However, I am again compelled to tell you that she didn't mean it, just as my stepdad did not mean to hurt me or to abuse me. I just can't tell you that they abused me without telling you that they didn't mean to do it, they are not at fault.

Brad, on the other hand, learned to deaden his feelings. His response at this early stage of the work is almost entirely intellectual. He wrote:

You told me that I am critical and rejecting and pretending not to be. I feel hopeless about my ability to get in touch with the ways in which I'm doing that. I don't think I'm holding back things, but I don't seem to be able to see or recognize what's going on inside me, or to get in touch with my resistances and defenses.

Each of these different reactions is based on fear—the fear of rejection or punishment we felt when we were children. But though appeasing, becoming hostile, or deadening, our selves may handle the fear for the moment, none of them extinguish the helplessness we experienced. They only disguise it. As a result, many of us spend much of our lives reacting to other people with hostility or appeasement or withholding, sometimes all at once. We all have seen someone angrily refuse to communicate with the very person whose affection they most desire.

The group session

After everyone in the group has listened to the feedback tape from their teacher, Ron asks them, "What was hardest to hear?" In answering that question, the group members again must focus on the patterns in their lives that are causing them the greatest difficulty. As they do, the teachers accept the reality of each person's experience and encourage them to see it in a new way.

Diane is prompt to speak, and somewhat tearful. "The hardest thing for me to hear was when Dorothea said that I can have either my parents or myself—that I can't have both."

"It's true, though." Ron assures her. "There is no way that you can keep your present relationship with your parents and realize your own true nature. And that is hard for the child inside of you to accept." He turns to the class. "Haven't some of you noticed that your child wants to change so that you can phone your parents and say 'Did I do it right? Will you accept me, now?' That's not real change."

The vital need for separation

The pain in our lives comes from the patterns we learned from our parents—but the reason we are stuck with them is that we still want our parents (or parent substitutes) to take care of us, to do it for us, to convince us that we are okay. This is true whether our parents are living or dead, for in either case it is our childhood image of them that we cling to, and that we so often project on to anyone else whom we see as being even momentarily important to us. We continue to be emotionally dependent on our parents until we are able to fully and consciously make the choice to separate ourselves from them and claim our own lives.

The group session

Larry, whose thin bearded face seldom shows expression or

involvement, speaks next. "What was hardest for me was when Kathy got so angry on my tape about the way my father beat me when I was a kid, and I realized that I didn't feel anything at all when I wrote that. You'd think I'd have some kind of emotional reaction, wouldn't you?"

Remembering his written notes about his childhood, Kathy asks him directly, "Why did you take the belt he used on you to your room and practice hitting yourself with it, Larry?"

He hesitates as the class goes still with a kind of shock, for they have not spoken much of violent physical abuse yet. His voice is detached. "I just wanted to get so he couldn't hurt me when he did it."

"You were so desperate when you were a boy that you beat yourself with a belt so that you could learn not to feel it when he did it!" The intensity and outrage in Kathy's voice reaches out to him. "Does that help you understand why you can't respond to anything except with deadness now?"

There is a brief silence as the group begins to understand the grim experiences that lie behind Larry's withdrawn attitude. He looks around slowly. "You know, I thought I'd feel humiliated to talk about that in front of the people in here. But I feel like they are on my side, not feeling contemptuous of me, like I thought the whole world was doing."

Kathy nods, "Right. Because your father sneered at you when you were a child you think the whole world is laughing at you. You think, 'I can't say what's true for me because they'll be contemptuous of me.' But you refused to stay trapped in your childhood when you took a chance and told us what happened. Good for you."

"There is another thing, though," Ron put in. "What if somebody did laugh? Maybe they are laughing because they are scared, or because they are being inappropriate. Sometimes other people aren't capable of supporting you; they are into their own struggles. Everybody isn't always going to support you in being yourself. But you'll all be surprised how much support you get when you give them a chance." Larry glances quickly at several of the other members as he nods. Their eyes meet his with warmth and friendliness.

44

An older man, his gray beard unexpected against the brown hair, has spoken little so far. Charlie is a professor at one of the state colleges and very much in control of himself. He says thoughtfully, "What was hardest for me was to hear that my mother, who was very quiet, was just as guilty as my father, who was angry all the time. I kept thinking I hadn't any reason to be angry at her, until I realized that I used to be angry because she never stood up for me to my father. And I don't complain to my wife, either, no matter how outrageous she is being. Not until I finally get mad and just explode."

Ron suggests, "It sounds like you go from being like your passive mother to acting out your angry father. And I'd guess that not only you don't stand up for yourself till you explode, but you don't trust women much to be there when you need them, since she wasn't." Again, there is a pause as the point sinks in.

Kathleen's voice is choked as she says, "The hardest thing for me to hear was about my father. I was really close to him till about the fourth grade, when he left. My teacher said on the tape that when that happened I believed that I hadn't been a good enough girl to keep him from leaving us. So I'm still trying to be a good girl now, and not ever feeling like I'm good enough. It really hit me. I know that's what happened. And it still happens with every other man in my life today. I always feel like I can't be good enough to keep them."

The anxiety of the group members rises as the continuing work brings their earlier experiences back into clearer focus. "Do you know how hard it is to go back to your childhood?" Arnold explodes. "I don't even want to think about what my childhood was like. And most of all, I don't want to feel like I did then."

Ron responds soberly, "Did you ever notice how often you give yourself the same kind of messages you got from your parents: 'I don't want to hear about your sadness.' 'I don't want to hear about your anger.' 'Don't be sad, don't be angry, don't feel this, don't feel that.' Our feelings don't go away because we don't want to feel them. They just go underground, get distorted, and find another way to surface.

"We need to have enough space for our pain and our anger to be heard. Until we can say what it was really like for us, it's very hard to move on in our lives. Part of us is still stuck back there, treating ourselves the way we were treated, and setting it up for other people to treat us that way too. Often we even think we deserve to be treated that way—ignored, beaten, abandoned, or smothered. But part of this work is to reclaim our childhood, because there is more than pain back there. For most of us that is where most of our joy and passion is buried, too."

The members of the group listen thoughtfully. The pace is slow as they continue to talk about what they found hard to accept on their feedback tapes. Tom says, "The thing that hit me hardest was about my being like a porcupine in dealing with people. I think of it as being a reaction to what they are doing, but maybe it is my pattern. That's not easy to think about. I always hated the way my mother was real touchy and hard to get along with."

Brad says grimly, "Kathy said that I've avoided achieving things because my father let me know early on that I'd better not compete with him. I never saw it that way before, but it's true. He put me down whatever I tried to do. I feel as if I pissed away my life, and for what? He just thinks I'm a bum. And I hate myself for being a failure."

Lily seems desperate. "All those bad things about my mother, I don't want to hear them. I know they are true, but she's my mother. I never say anything bad about her at all. I don't know what would happen."

Marion asks, "Do you know that when abused children are asked, 'Why did your mother hit you?' they never say, 'Because she's bad.' They say, 'Because I was bad.' That's the only thing that makes sense to them. Father and mother are a little child's whole world; they make everything go around. It's better to think that you are wrong and bad than that your whole world is wrong and bad. It's less terrifying.

"Besides," she continued, "if you are the one that is bad, there is some hope that you might change yourself and be good. But if you realize that your father beats you any time he feels like it, or that your mother just can't be bothered with you, you feel totally helpless. The tragedy is that you have learned to believe that you are the one who is bad and wrong."

Cheryl recognizes that pattern in herself. "I felt that way all my life.

Maybe if I could figure out how to change myself, they wouldn't treat me so bad. I felt responsible for what happened."

Margie whispers, "It was hard to hear things on the tape I would have been punished for even daring to think about my parents when I was little. Besides, they were very responsible people."

"Responsible for making you miserable for most of your life," Dorothea responds firmly.

Ron ends that part of the session on a note of comfort. "There is a lot of strength in letting yourself feel that vulnerability. And I want you all to realize that if you survived it once, you can survive the memory of it. You have a lot more resources now, and you are no longer alone. You've already made a shift in opening this painful stuff up for discussion.

"But it is also time for you to begin looking for new possibilities in your daily lives, and trying them out," he continues. "All the way through this work you will have a choice—to stay with the ways you learned to protect yourself or to try something new. You can start to ask yourself, 'What am I doing that I always do? How did I learn to do that? Do I punish myself for what I see, or do I just acknowledge that it is happening? And, what happens if I experiment with doing something different?'"

Arnold demands glumly, "But what if you try to do something different, and it comes out just the way it always does? That's why I don't keep trying. It just doesn't work. I psych myself up to go into a social situation and tell myself that this time things will be different, but I still end up by myself, having a rotten time. So I feel like it's just a waste."

"Did your parents teach you comfort and ease in such situations?"

Arnold's laugh is harsh. "No way."

Ron says, "You can't force yourself to be a way you didn't learn to be. But you can become aware of what you are doing from one moment to the next that keeps things the same, and begin to experiment a little at a time with doing something different.

"When you are in a social situation, watch what you are telling yourself about what is going on. Watch the lack of respect for yourself and the self-sabotage you learned. You want friends, but how friendly are you to yourself? How might you act if you were really committed to your own well-being?

"The essential part of you, your spirit, wants your life to be different and real." Ron tells them. "And then there is your programmed emotional child claiming, 'This is too hard; it makes me feel bad,' and your programmed intellect coming in with 'See, I told you. Nothing is going to change this time either.' You need to decide who you are going to listen to, and what you are going to do about it.

"And I am not not urging you to push and strain and grunt. I'm urging you to be here for yourself and for this work. Only you can do it. We can show you the door and even help you pry it open, but only you can walk through it—one step at a time."

Chapter Three Exercises

Remember, you are working with your childhood images, not with your parents of today. No matter how things begin to look to you while you are working with this book, do not get involved in blame, recriminations, etc., with your living parents. To do so will hinder, not help, your efforts on your own behalf. Also watch that you don't transfer whatever feelings may arise onto significant others currently in your life. And don't get involved in feeling guilty about how you have treated any children you may have. This work is about your own inner child. As you change, a change for the better becomes natural in all your relationships.

Ask yourself the following questions and note the answers in your journal or put them on tape.

Exercise 1

a. If someone was giving you honest and straightforward feedback on your responses to the book and the exercises so far, what would you be afraid of hearing (that you are too mousy, too angry, or something else)? Would you let yourself hear any negative feedback?

b. What about feedback on the positive aspects of yourself that are showing up? Could you let yourself hear feedback on your strengths? What are they? List a few.

c. How do you typically respond to feedback in your life: with openness, fear, resentment, or something else?

d. Look at the responses of each group member to the feedback they got. Which one touched you most deeply? What does that suggest about your life and your childhood relationship with your parents?

Exercise 2

a. Imagine yourself driving down the highway and being pulled over by a policeman, or remember when that actually happened. Was your response that of an appeaser (guilty and subservient), a hostile (angry and resentful), or a withholder (no reaction at all)?

b. Do you often automatically react like that in the rest of your life? Do you sometimes act out the other two positions?

c. In which of these categories would you put each of your parents?

d. Can you see how you learned your way of reacting as an appeaser, a hostile or a withholder from your parents?

(You may be copying them or rebelling against their usual way of behaving. If you copied them, you will either be doing as they did to others, doing it to yourself, or expecting others to do it to you. If you rebelled, you are stuck with doing the opposite of whatever they did.)

Remember, having these thoughts and writing down negative material or putting it on tape will not hurt your parents. You are not creating negative imagery, but working with what already exists in either your conscious or unconscious mind. Recognizing it is a way of telling the truth and will help free you from the past.

Stage II: Anger

Chapter Four: The Way It Really Was

Bringing the past into focus

The group now begins to investigate their childhood years systematically, often through the use of imagery. What were holidays like, they are asked, and how about the first day of school? What happened around the dinner table, and at bedtime? What messages did they get about sex? Until they relive these moments in detail, the members do not remember and cannot even imagine how strongly they felt as children when they did not get the love and approval they needed.

They are asked to write descriptions of dozens of such scenes as if they were happening to them right now, giving them as much emotional reality as possible. As they do, they begin to recognize how their needs were being ignored, their tenderest feelings trampled on, and their belief in themselves destroyed. They can see how often they were frightened, hurt, and angry.

As they explore their childhoods, they find that blatantly traumatic happenings are far from the whole story. Daily learnings in hundreds of connected incidents also drove the early lessons deeply and bitterly home. Sometimes they describe events that appear to be unimportant, banal, or neutral. It is only when they consider what they were actually learning that they see its serious consequences. They see that even the most ordinary event can carry a destructive message.

For instance, perhaps father's threatening growl was a common occurrence. It was intended to frighten us into the behavior he wanted us to exhibit. At that moment, he really didn't know or care whether we learned to cringe inside, if only we would learn not to bother him when he wanted to watch a football game on TV. Similarly, perhaps mother's immaculate kitchen was more important to her than the fact that it was the first time the other kids were willing to come to our house. It was our chance finally to be accepted as one of the gang, but she wouldn't let us bring them in. Her attitude taught us how little our emotional needs mattered to her, and as a consequence, how little they should mean to us.

This theme of noncaring has a thousand variations, from those that seem inconsequential in most adult eyes to those that are abusive by almost any standards. When these recognitions are encouraged to surface without restriction, without the need to invalidate our experience by trying to consider our parents' side of it, a sense of relief and honesty arises. We can finally let ourselves admit that is how it was, and that is how it felt. For we cannot feel in our hearts all of the painful emotions of childhood while, at the same time, holding in our heads that our parents loved us to the best of their ability. The attempt to do so often creates a sort of internal paralysis—an inability to understand what is going on within us and to deal fully with our early feelings.

Consciously looking for what was wrong

In one of Cheryl's initial descriptions of her mother, she tried to protect her from criticism, and to emphasize her positive aspects.

> *My mother was an emotional person. She was full of warmth and lots of affection toward us. She liked to hug and kiss all of her children. She was creative and liked to do a lot of fun things with us. I do remember her being angry more often than anything else. She was a high-strung person and she would express herself by yelling and screaming a lot. She would throw things around and sometimes hit us with whatever she had in her hand, especially me because I was the oldest and she wanted me to learn to be responsible for the others.*

*She treated my father with respect, but also with a sense
of always needing to show him the correct way to do things.
She would tell him how to eat, sleep, run his business, and
even how to feel. She dictated to all of us our chores, even my
father when he was home. She would tell us what the world
was about and how we should view situations. She was very
protective and involved with us.*

While all of these things may be true, focusing on mother's positive features is not useful in the early part of the Process. The time for Cheryl to appreciate the good aspects of her mother will come later. Defending her mother at this stage will prevent her from fully acknowledging the destructiveness of some of the messages she received, and readying herself to deal with those messages and with her dependency on her mother.

Cheryl first needs to confront the negativities in both her parents straight on. She needs to see what it meant to her as a little child to have an untrustworthy mother who was loving at times, but at other times yelled and screamed and threw things at the children (especially her). She needs to recognize the messages she received about the relationship between men and women when she saw her mother always needing to show her father "the correct way to do things," and telling her whole family how they should "view situations."

Complex learnings

Many of the group members do not have clear memories of their childhood. They have forgotten much of what happened to them and how it affected them. They have repressed such memories to avoid the painful emotions originally connected with them. Mother may have slapped them, and they remember feeling hurt and bewildered. Further along in the work they will remember that they were also angry and wanted to hit back. For others, the situation was reversed. Anger was admissible in the family, but hurt and bewilderment were disapproved as signs of weakness.

As they are helped to examine the scenes in their childhood through writing and reliving scenes, the members of the group begin to realize how complex their negative learnings were. They each had mother and father images to deal with. This is true even though there never was any kind of father figure around, for children's fantasies of their missing fathers have lifelong repercussions. Furthermore, each of their parents or parent substitutes were complicated human beings. Each parent wanted different things from them at different times, and sometimes even at the same time.

Some of the members had managed to retain a somewhat positive view of themselves, in spite of their parents' negativity and distance. In such cases, there almost inevitably was a grandmother or grandfather or other person whom they remembered fondly as "the one who really cared." Fortunate as this influence was, it caused other problems, because the one who really cared probably had little actual say in the total life of the child. As a result, loving acceptance became linked in their minds with lack of power, and as adults they tended to devaluate anyone who loved them.

Children in the same family are treated differently

The childhood situations of the members become clearer as they are examined in different ways. Diane maintains that her difficulties cannot have been rooted in her upbringing. Her twin sister, Nancy, doesn't have problems in self-esteem as she does. Nancy was always the leader, a confident and popular child, while Diane trailed behind her. In her notes, Diane wrote:

> *I've always had a terrible self-image, and it's my fault. There is something wrong with me. Our parents always treated us the same, dressed us the same, gave us the same toys, took us to the same places, all that.*

Diane's mystery begins to unravel when the group is asked to bring in childhood photographs, so that the attitudes of family members can be recognized from their postures and expressions. Several of Diane's photographs show the twins with a cheerfully smiling mother—the smile and her whole body inclined toward Nancy, while Diane stands disconsolately by, clinging to her mother's other hand.

As her childhood memories emerge more clearly, Diane recognizes that treating both twins exactly the same outwardly did not change the reality that Nancy had been her mother's favorite from the days when Diane was sickly as a baby. (Most mothers favor the sickly child, but Diane's mother had a sickly younger sister who got all her parents' attention and still resented her.)

Perhaps reacting to the special connection between their mother and Nancy, their father made Diane his favorite. It was the mother, however, who was the competent, outgoing, dominant partner, while the father had tended to be withdrawn, insecure and nervous. Each child had identified more and more with the parent who accepted them most fully.

As the pieces begin to fit together, Diane begins to comprehend what the teachers mean by saying "You were innocent. You learned the patterns you are living out." She begins to consider the possibility that there really isn't anything fundamentally wrong with her.

Siblings are treated differently in almost all families. Sometimes, the disparate treatment is because of differences in birth order, in gender, or in the family situation at the time they were born. Sometimes, a particular child reminds the mother or father of one of their parents, or of a favored or hated brother or sister. Feelings about this relationship are transferred to their child. For children so identified, the sense of reality is strongly disturbed. They constantly face subtle demands and reactions that are related, not actually to them, but to a figure from their parent's past.

Often, boys are strongly favored by mothers who have accepted the tradition of male importance. On the other hand, many boys have suffered inordinately because of their mother's unconscious anger over that same fact. And how can a woman who feels bitterness and resentment toward men teach her daughters to feel good about themselves as women, or to feel loving and trustful toward men?

A seemingly positive childhood

In one of the early sessions, Mike says he isn't sure he has anything to be angry about because his childhood was quite happy. He came from an intact family, and his mother was always home and available to her four children. His father, though strict, was a fair and decent man. He remembers having lots of fun as a boy, playing with his brothers and his friends.

As an adult, however, Mike cannot acknowledge his own feelings or handle the feelings of his wife and children. He knows he is often angry inside while outwardly being compliant and dutiful. Gradually, he is becoming aware that he is afraid that people will think he is bad if he is honest about his feelings, or they will be hurt and leave him. He is still not much in contact with his emotions, but he is beginning to make some connections between his childhood and his adult experiences. He describes his father during his middle childhood years.

> *Dad is tense, unhappy, and angry most of the time, but he never expresses it honestly. He is busy all the time at his office, with earning enough money to support us, with his church and club work, with his lectures. That leaves him feeling tired all the time, not ever being able to relax or play or to spend any time with us. I think he resents that, but he never says so, and it's always like he's being dutiful. He never tells Mother or us what he's angry about (he just hums a lot). It seems like he and Mother are always angry at each other, but they never fight. I often feel the tension and unhappiness in this house. I escape and play outside with my friends whenever I can.*

Negative childhood scenes with mother

As they write more and more scenes, the group members' understanding of what had happened to them deepens. Judy recognizes herself as a pleaser who needs people to like her so much that she immediately puts aside her own wants and desires in favor of someone else's. She is also unable to handle anger and is always trying to smooth things over so that no one will get angry.

She wrote a simple scene about a time when she was three, three years before her mother actually died and thus abandoned her completely. She speaks as a child might, and her language captures the need she feels to refashion herself to please her mother.

> *I have spilled my milk again and Mommy is angry and she won't talk to me. It feels awful. I mustn't spill my milk any more so Mommy will love me. But I do other things, too. She*

was mad at me yesterday because Billy and I were making so much noise. We were both being very bad. Mommy gets real mad when we make trouble for her, and then she doesn't want us around her. I have to learn to be good so Mommy can love me.

In the notes Margie turned in, she admitted that when people act loving and affirming toward her, she feels that they are hiding their negative feelings about her. It is hard for her to accept compliments or statements of affection because she never believes they are sincere. Also, she feels fake when she says positive things to people, even though she means them. She believes that people think she is insincere and know that deep inside she is a bitter, critical person. She wrote of a scene when she was five.

I know that Mom talks bad about other people, even Daddy and Gramma, and puts them down behind their backs, but I know she has only love for me, and she would never talk about me that way. It has never even occurred to me that she might. I am the one person in the world who is exempt.

Mom walks out the kitchen door to go sit on the steps of her friend Mary's porch next door and talk. A minute later, I decide to go out, too, and go sit on the bottom step of the porch with her and wrap my arms and legs around her leg like I like to do. I get as far as the corner of Mary's house and I hear Mom saying to Mary, "Do you know what that stupid little jerk of a kid just did? She just . . ." and she describes something I've just done.

I stop walking. I can hardly believe it. I get a big lump in my throat and another big lump in my stomach. I go sit in the backyard alone. I am too stunned to even cry. I feel like my whole world has caved it. Now I am one of the rotten people in the world, and I will never again really be sure what Mom thinks of me.

As Margie relives this deep loss and longing, she begins to understand that the child within her is still feeling left out, vulnerable, and bitter. With this childhood memory she begins to sense an enormous yearning within her—the unfulfilled yearning for her mother's full approval and love.

Our early learnings occurred in a deeply emotional context, and we cannot know their full importance to us unless those emotions are aroused once more. We need to re-enter the times of fear and confusion, of loneliness and despair we lived through as children. Only in this way can we realize how great was the pressure that drove us to create the false self we live with today.

Feeling the need for mother's love

When we are angry at our parents, there is always grief under the anger—grief over losing the earliest and deepest love of our lives. If this grief and despair is not recognized, our anger and in fact our whole lives will remain superficial. We are denying part of our own experience, and therefore we do not know ourselves.

A special session on childhood longing and grief for mother is held at this point. The more deeply the group members re-experience the hunger of the unfulfilled child within them, the better they will understand how desperately they needed mother's unconditional love, and why they were willing to become whatever she wanted in order to try to gain it.

They have been asked to bring to this session pads, blankets, or sleeping bags to lie on. They know in advance only that they are going to do some work with their images of their mothers. (The work with mother is done separately from the work with father. They are different people, and the child's relationship with each of them is different.) The members are subdued, sensing that the painful feelings and realizations they are having are likely to become even stronger. Some are worried that they won't be able to feel as deeply as they need to. A few are still distrustful that they are going to be manipulated in some way.

The room is darkened, and pensive classical music plays softly in the background. The teachers are quiet as they direct the group members to lie on their pads side by side, leaving a few feet of space between them. Just lying down on the floor while the teachers are standing (which makes them seem very big) begins to bring back

early feelings. This session is planned to give each of the members of the group an opportunity to feel the need, the helplessness, and the sense of bottomless yearning for love and acceptance they felt when they were very young.

After they lie quietly for a while, listening to the music, Ron asks them all to sit up and give the people on each side of them permission to do or feel whatever they need to, and to make any kind of sound they need to make. Many touch hands, or hug each other as they whisper their permission, before lying down again. This brief connection makes it easier for each of them to stop worrying about what the others may think of them.

Kathy begins to speak to the group now, reassuring them that whatever they experience is all right, that there is no need to accomplish or achieve anything, and that they can just be open to whatever happens. She talks about how alone they felt when they were very young, and how often they had learned to swallow back their pain and tears. She tells them it is now necessary to let themselves feel that pain and let those tears out.

She speaks of how each of them came into the world as beautiful, open, sensitive babies, full of hope and expectation and joy, reaching out with love to be accepted, to be nourished, to be loved unconditionally, to feel totally safe in the arms of the most important woman in their lives—their own mothers. She talks of how none of them were really fulfilled in that need, and how terribly abandoned they felt. Her voice brimming with compassion, she speaks of how all that longing and loss are still affecting them today—how they still can't believe in their hearts that they really deserve to be loved.

As the group members lie in the dark listening to the emotionally moving words and music, the other teachers spend time with each of them separately. The teachers encourage them to breathe deeply, touching them, sometimes holding them and becoming the loving mother for whom they yearned when they were small. Cheryl begins to whimper in a heartbroken, childish tone of voice. One of the men cries out; a harsh, strangled sound. Ron goes to him and wraps his arms around him and rocks him. All around the room, people begin to experience the sense of early loss and sorrow, and some break into sobs. Elaine, however, lies stiffly inside her sleeping bag, and Dorothea strokes her hair lightly, knowing she is not ready to let herself be held.

Marion speaks after a time, asking the group to listen to her words with their hearts, to let themselves go back still deeper into those early years, to get in touch with the fragile, vulnerable child within. Still later, Dorothea takes her turn, describing a mother whose love did not have to be earned, but whose heart overflows naturally and spontaneously with love for her family, who takes joy in each thing that happens to them, who feels that each one is special and of infinite value—always ending on the note, "But your mother wasn't like that, was she?"

Kathy is sitting with Brad. At last he begins to tremble with the emotions he has held back so long. As she holds him and whispers the words of endearment he wanted so desperately to hear from his mother, he clings to her tightly and a few tears course down his cheeks. He is letting go to feelings he ruled out of his life many years ago. It is one of the important turning points in his work.

Marion is now with Elaine, who is curled up against her—not sobbing, but not resisting either. For Elaine, too, this is an important shift. Later she wrote:

> *When I realized that this was going to be a crying session, I felt stiff and resistant. When the first woman started crying, I could feel myself stiffen more. I didn't like her sobbing. Come on, control yourself, I thought (and where does that voice come from, I asked myself sarcastically). I found it hard to have a sense of myself as a child. Everyone else's crying distracted me. The man on my left started almost howling. I hated that sound. (Men are not to cry, and certainly not to cry like that, the voice said). I felt helpless. He made me think of lying in bed, listening to my brothers cry while Mom yelled at them and hit them, and not being able to do anything but numb myself out.*
>
> *I was pretty much withdrawn from the whole scene when Marion sat down beside me. When she lifted me up and started rocking me, my first reaction was "don't—don't."*

Then I started to cry, but I pressed my clenched fist against my mouth to keep it contained. I was crying almost grudgingly. I felt like I was giving in to the sorrow, but not all the way.

Most of the others are able to experience more fully the early feelings of grief and loss they have warded off for so long. Peter wrote:

The beginning of the session was difficult. I was pretty uptight and I didn't know what to expect. But as the teachers went on talking and the music played I really felt my child. I began to feel how alone and neglected I was then and how I'd been made to act like a grown-up way too early, instead of ever being Mommy's baby. I felt how I shut down when things happened that I couldn't handle. I cried and sobbed and shook down to my absolute core. All the locked up stuff just poured out.

It was so wonderful to finally be held and loved and understood just for me. It felt like the kind of dedicated, caring love that I never received. When we stood on our feet at the end, everybody looked different. We're all in this together and we're all ready to go for it. Everybody was hugging each other and I especially hugged the guy next to me who I used to think was a jerk. It was the most cleansing experience I've ever had.

Longing for father

The mood of the group changes when they move on to father. There is a strange kind of tension, and laughter that is too quick and a bit forced. The members know by this time that their fathers are terribly important to them, but the extent to which they have been shaped by their relationship with him is still largely unknown. Clearly, it is beginning to feel like an ominous unknown to many of them.

No matter how angry they might have been at their mothers, they felt connected to her in some way. They always knew that what they really wanted in their mothers was a warm, gentle, loving, accepting, nourishing presence. But they weren't quite sure what they wanted from their fathers. Love and acceptance, yes, but in what form? What is a father supposed to be like?

For many of them, the relationship with their fathers had been so tenuous, so absent, that negative childhood scenes with him were difficult to write. They often had to describe scenes of omission, the times father should have been there for them but wasn't—the laughter, the sharing, the quiet cuddling that didn't happen, the school events he didn't attend, the needed support that was not given. Often, too, he was the man who was not emotionally available, even though he may have been physically present.

In the absence of an emotional connection, a child hears that he or she doesn't deserve attention, that he or she isn't important enough to matter to this man who seems so powerful and godlike. The people in the group feel that somehow they are lacking. In their hearts they still believe that their fathers had something to give that would have made them feel strong and free and safe in the world—and he had not found them worthy of this gift.

Ann wrote of a scene with her father when she was not quite five.

> *Daddy is going to the store. I beg to go along and he says no until Mommy tells him take me along because she wants a nap. I love to go to the store with Daddy even though I have to run very fast to keep up with him, and I mustn't stop and look at things. On our way out of the store after the shopping is done, they have a horse you can put money in and you can ride. I ask Daddy if I can ride the horse, please. Daddy says, "No, I don't have time today."*
>
> *I remember once, a long time ago, I got to ride the horse. But I don't get to ride it anymore, he always says no. I really loved it that time I was on the horse and he stood beside me while I rode. But Mommy says I mustn't bug him, or he won't ever take me with him, so I am good and I don't ask again. Why isn't there ever enough time for anything?*

Other group members remembered their fathers as a strong presence, but an almost entirely negative one. What they remember is a harsh and angry man, or perhaps a weak and worthless one. Still, they yearned for him when they were children.

Charlie claims that he had no feeling other than contempt for the alcoholic father who deserted his mother and him when he was a boy. He grew up to think of himself as extremely self-sufficient. He was unwilling to permit himself any experience of need or dependency. A memory of a different kind came to him one evening while he was working on his homework.

For a long time I can't make any order out of my thoughts. My mind keeps going blank when I even try to remember what he looked like. And then I begin to get this sense of him standing by the door of the house we lived in when I was little. He looks big and strong and exciting. I am a little kid, filled with love and admiration for him. I don't care how my mother feels about him. I want him to know he can count on me. I'll be there waiting when he comes back. I'll hold the fort for him! The image fades, and I'm an adult again, with that familiar empty, lost feeling inside.

Though the format in the father grief session is the same as for mother, the words Marion uses to help the members really feel the wounds of their childhood are different. "Let yourself feel it. Beneath the walls that you had to build around your heart, there was a tender, vulnerable place where you wanted your father. Where was he while you were growing up? 'Daddy, I want you to show me that you love me and you want to be with me. I feel like I don't matter to you, Daddy. Why don't you like me? Is there something wrong with me? I'm trying so hard to be good!'"

Kathy talks about how natural it is to want your father's attention, to want to be important to him, to want to feel his strong support and caring. One of our most basic needs is to be able to feel what we need from life. "Your father," he tells the group, "hid his needs and didn't want to hear about yours. He didn't want to hear how much you wanted him to hold you and love you and really see you. And you took his message deep into your heart: ignore your own needs, cover them up, give up expecting anything—and pretend you don't feel despair because your father doesn't really care about you."

Dorothea tells them, "It's all right to feel. Feelings come like waves in the ocean, in and out. One wave after another of all the pain and longing you have held back all your life long. The yearning for all the things that could have been between you. The sadness because he wasn't there for you." Once again, the people in the group are able to let go in their different ways into the longing and grief they felt as little children.

After an hour or so, Ron introduces another possibility. They have experienced their feelings of sadness and loss deeply. They have had the strength to look at what happened to them—at how the lack of love from their mothers and fathers has caused their hearts to close up, to retreat behind the wall they built to protect themselves. They know what that wall has cost them. He suggests that now it is possible to go beyond those feelings to a new potential within their hearts. They do not have to live the rest of their lives behind walls, tight and constricted. There are other possibilities, other worlds. They can release the child within them from all that holding and pain, so that they can embrace the world as they were meant to.

"Feel that possibility growing in you," he tells them. "A new possibility born of releasing the old pain and opening to something new and fresh. As you feel that potential now, slowly let yourself stand up." When the whole group is standing, Ron brings them into a circle where they can see each other. Again there is new softness and warmth and understanding, a felt movement still deeper into compassion for themselves and for each other.

Afterwards, Ann wrote:

> *When Ron said we could make a choice about how we felt now, I felt a ray of light from my Spirit shooting throughout my body and I felt incredibly strong and beautiful from inside. In that moment I really got a sense of myself without the monkey on my back. When I looked around the room I saw the most beautiful faces. The masks had been shed. Feelings were being shown. Pain was out there to be seen and felt. There was such a glow of realness and humanness in the faces of these people I am coming to know as I have never known anyone in my life before.*

Chapter Four Exercises

At this stage of the Process you may be learning much that you find difficult to accept about yourself and about your parents. Be gentle with yourself, treat yourself with as much care and tenderness as possible. You are trying to see the truth, not blame yourself for it. Whatever you are doing today is a reaction to what you learned when you were very young, and were helpless to do anything else. Remember, though, if you are becoming unduly anxious, you should stop doing the exercises, or else continue with them with the help of a therapist familiar with the issues raised in this book.

Even if much of your childhood was positive (and it had to have some positive aspects in it or you wouldn't have survived to read this book) there was much that was negative (or you wouldn't be reading this book, either). You are not being disloyal to your parents, you are being loyal to yourself.

Ask yourself these questions and note the answers in your journal or put them on tape.

Exercise 1

a. Think of the general flavor of your own childhood. Were you mostly quiet and dreamy, studious, hyperactive, defiant, compliant, fearful?

b. Which parent seems to be the most significant in your childhood? Did that change at different ages? Can you let yourself recognize that both of your parents had an enormous effect on your life, even if they were not physically (or emotionally) there for you?

Exercise 2

Add as many more negative traits as you can think of now to the three you found for each parent in the second exercise in Chapter 1. Write down also the negative messages they gave you (either verbally or silently).

Exercise 3

    a. Write out the most important negative childhood scenes you remember in which your mother and father were demonstrating their negative traits and/or giving you negative messages about yourself and the world. The scenes may be about unfairness, misunderstanding, grief, abuse, neglect, or any aspect of your childhood that brought you pain. Be specific, use details, try to write as if your child was holding the pen. (See the examples given in the middle of Chapter 4.) Write down at least a couple of scenes for each.

    b. As you look at your scenes, did you write them as if one of your parents was holding the pen, or can you identify with your child's pain, confusion or anger?

    c. How would you feel if you saw someone treating another child as you were treated?

    d. Note what you were learning about yourself and the world in each scene, and how those beliefs, feelings and behavior are affecting you today.

    For instance, were you learning that you weren't worth your fathers time? In that case, how worthy of other people's time and attention do you feel today? Were you learning that it is a terrible thing to make a mistake? In that case, are you afraid of trying new things today because you might make a mistake, and are you terribly upset when you make one? Did you feel truly loved? If you didn't, do you feel loved today? Are you able to love as you would like to?

Exercise 4

    Were you moved by the group sessions on the feeling the need for mother's and father's love and full acceptance? How do you imagine you might feel if you let yourself experience the depth of your childhood longing for unconditional love from your mother? Your father?

Chapter Five: Confronting Mother

Anger as a resource

Anger is an almost indispensable tool in arousing the strength we need to break out of the beliefs about ourselves and the world that we learned when we were children. Unleashed, righteous anger, directed specifically against the mental images that keep us fearful, inadequate, unloving, and unloved, can work magic in freeing us to affirm our real selves.

Anger is a powerful, active, assertive energy. It can cause great harm or, wisely directed, can lead to freedom and self-expression. We can use our anger not to hurt ourselves or others but to overcome our own fear and numbness and phoniness. We need to acknowledge our anger, and channel the aggressive action that can so easily arise from it. What matters is our intention. If we try to hold on to anger and keep building it because we think we are justified in doing so, or because we can't imagine any other situation, then we will continue to live with it. If our intention is to work through the anger and come into our own strength and reality, then that is what will happen.

The full expression of anger at our parents must be carefully focused if it is to serve us in this way. It should be experienced in powerful imagery, rather than at our actual mothers and fathers (or anyone else). Anger that is acted out against people in our current lives is almost always misplaced and destructive.

Anger is the only alternative children have to placating or going numb when they feel punished or abandoned by their parents. Childhood anger, though, is largely powerless. It may have some effect, but it is not the one the child really wants—which is to feel valuable and loved.

From the beginning, our anger is usually either falsified or repressed. False anger is anger that is directed at the wrong target, in the wrong amount, or for the wrong reasons. It blinds us to reality and perspective. False anger strengthens the "I'm right, you're wrong" syndrome, forcing us to see the target (often ourselves) as wrong and evil. Repressed anger is a poison, and causes us enormous stress. Furthermore, repressed anger always "leaks out" in some way to spoil our relationships with other people and with ourselves.

Acknowledged anger gives us the ability to demand justice, and the energy to sustain action until victory is achieved. The unreserved acknowledgment and safe expression of anger accesses our strength and makes possible awareness and honesty in our feelings and attitudes. It can arouse us from apathy, defeat, and depression, and put us in contact with the power and direction we need to change our lives.

Acknowledged anger is a transition point between being a fearful victim and the experience of power and mastery. One of the first steps on the road to true spirituality is the recognition that we are not victims, that we have choices, and that our choices make an enormous difference in our lives.

For these reasons, the members of the group are given the opportunity to fully experience their anger and express it in a totally safe and supportive environment.

Rising anger in the group

In the next session the members continue to investigate and get rightfully indignant about the beliefs about themselves and the world they learned from their mothers. (They will work with their mothers first, since she came first in their lives.) The teachers point out vividly how these learnings spoiled the happiness of their childhoods, and still are affecting them destructively today.

By now, almost all of the members are seeing how much they have to be angry about, but they still need a lot of support in expressing their anger. Depending on the kind of programming they received in childhood, they may be afraid of not doing it right, of looking silly, of offending somebody, or of losing control of themselves.

The teachers deliberately encourage the rising anger, dealing with each objection and hesitancy as it is expressed. The group members continue to bring up what is hardest for them to accept in what they are learning about themselves and their mothers. What is hardest to accept is apt to be what there is to be most angry about. Cheryl says, "One of the hardest things for me was when Kathy said my mother was an actress, and that all that self-sacrifice of hers was a facade. And that as a result I learned to be an actress, and outwardly to play good girl to get people's approval, and it's all an act, too. She hit that nail on the head, and it's scary to sit here and admit that."

Kathy asks her, "What are you really like under the smile and the act?"

"I'm dependent and I'm depressed and I'm angry, just like her."

Kathy nods, but puts a different slant on it. "That's not who you really are; that's who she taught you to believe that you are. That's what that actress of a mother did to you. You saw the pain in your face in those childhood pictures of yours we looked at last week. She did that to you, you didn't do it to yourself. But it's a good thing you have that anger, you can use it here to free yourself."

"It's really hard for me to direct my anger at her. It's a lot easier to get angry at my husband."

To make the pain in her relationship to her mother clearer to her, Ron encourages Cheryl to see the image of her mother in front of her and tell her forcefully how she feels about what happened when she was a child. After a few moments of rising indignation, her shoulders slump and she bursts into tears.

Kathy says, "It's okay to get angry and it's okay to cry. But you don't have to cry; you can just feel your own strength. You don't have to keep on acting like a victim. Something can change."

Nevertheless, Cheryl continues to sob. After a minute, Kathy tells her quietly to stop. She knows how easy it is for Cheryl to wallow in her tears and sense of being a victim, just as her mother had done.

"The pain is too easy for you. Just a moment ago you were feeling real outrage. It's just as real. You've been spewing that anger onto other people all your life in so many little insidious ways. It's time you put it where it belongs. Try saying, 'I don't have to be a lying, empty pretender like you, Mom.'"

Emboldened, Cheryl stops sobbing, takes a deep breath, and repeats the words, strongly and angrily. She looks surprised at her own expression of courage. Her face brightens.

Kathy tells her, "You've got gifts and talents you've never let yourself live out, because that role of victim is safe and easy and familiar. You deserve better than that."

"It's a bitter pill," Ron tells the class emphatically. "You are your mother! The sooner you see it, the sooner you can begin to move away from it. You either do everything to other people that she did, or you do it to yourself, or you expect other people to do it to you. That's the way you have become your mother." It is a point he has made before. Each session it takes on greater reality for each of them.

Mike is sitting very straight, his hands gripping the arms of his chair. He clearly wants to be angry and knows he needs to be angry, but his programming has recaptured him. "I still feel guilty when I let myself get angry at my folks," he says with frustration in his voice. "After all, the Bible says to honor your father and your mother!"

Marion presses him earnestly. "And how does it honor them to hang on to that resentment and hatred the rest of your life, while you pretend you don't feel it?"

"But if it's okay to get angry at them, why do I feel so guilty? And why do I feel so rotten when I feel guilty?" The emotional conflict in him is strong. The teachers are glad to see it surface, for he has been out of contact with his feelings for most of his life.

"When you do something your parents would disapprove of, you do what they did—you tell yourself you are a bad boy, and should be punished," Marion explains. "That's what you are doing to yourself at this moment. You are punishing yourself for wanting to be free of her influence by making yourself feel guilty and rotten. When you have really worked through your resentment and anger at your mother and father, you may be able to be a real son to them. Up

70

to now you've had to brush them off and stay away from them so that you don't act out how you really feel."

Turning to Lily, who is, as usual, huddled down in her chair, Ron asks her how she is doing.

She answers reluctantly, "I'm scared, I guess. But I also see how I project my mother on everybody. I don't see real people out there. I just see versions of her—I think everybody really despises me like she did."

Lily's mother had not only abused and terrified her, but convinced her that no one else would ever help her. The teachers know she needs to accept more support from the group. Dorothea says, "And she never wanted you to tell on her, did she? Are you willing to tell the group one of the scenes with her that you wrote, Lily?"

She mumbles, "I still feel like what happened in them is my fault."

"Yes, I know; she tried to convince you that you were bad, and that's why she treated you that way. When you were in your high chair and she wanted you to eat something you didn't want, what would she do?"

Lily looks down and whispers, "She'd tie my hands down and then she'd grab my hair to hold my head still and force the food in my mouth."

Everyone in the room feels a stab of pain for the little girl Lily had been, and still is. Dorothea goes on. "And she'd be really angry right now, wouldn't she, hearing you say this much?"

"I feel like she is here right in my head, telling me not to talk about what happened."

"She is. And you are fighting to get your own head back. So I want you to try one more thing. I want you to try standing up and telling everybody in the room, 'You're not my mother. Sometimes you look like her to me, but I know you are not.'"

Lily half stands and glances hesitantly around. Finally, a shy little smile breaks through the strained features. "I know you're not my mother," she tells them hurriedly, and slides back into her seat.

The others applaud her sympathetically and call out encouraging comments. They all know how hard even this small step is for her.

Ron turns to the group and says, "What it takes to change your life is to be willing to live it out in front of people instead of hiding yourself in a back room someplace. What you do out here will not be perfect; you will stumble. So what? That's what keeps you in those back rooms, because you weren't allowed to stumble when you were a child, or to just acknowledge the fact that you were learning."

Peter says, "I'm seeing things I've never been aware of before. I spent my whole life defending my mother. I can't believe that I'm feeling as angry and disgusted with her as I'm feeling. The things Marion said about my mother are right on, but I still can't believe them!"

"I didn't say anything that you didn't say in your notes," Marion points out. Remembering one of his scenes, she adds, "If you closed your eyes right now and saw your mother when you were four years old, doing what she was doing on that couch right in front of you, what would you say?"

Peter closes his eyes and lets himself become four years old as he relives the scene. After a moment, he almost whimpers, "Leave that guy alone. I don't want you to kiss that man like that. He's not my Daddy!"

"Can you tell your mother how it makes you feel?"

"Yeah, it hurts, and I want to tell Daddy on you, but I don't dare."

"Can you tell her how angry it makes you?"

Softly he says, "I just hate you." Persuaded by the teachers to try expressing himself more, he forces the words out louder and louder until he is almost shouting, "I hate you! I hate you!"

"How do you feel now?"

"A little better, but this is really hard for me. One of the things you told me on the tape is that I act like a little boy a lot of the time because that gets me what I want. Like I did with my mother to get what I wanted from her. And I'm scared to death to be angry at her."

Ron picks up the thread. "Close your eyes again and see your Mom. What would she do if you got angry at her? Would she get angry back?"

"Yeah, but in a real controlled way. She'd get this hard, scornful look on her face and say, 'You go to your room, you bad boy.' I spent half my childhood in my room."

Now Ron starts to act out an exaggerated version of Peter's mother. Harshly, he tells Peter, "What I do is none of your business, you rotten kid. You just be good and keep doing what I want you to, or else go to your room!"

Peter answers "no" weakly at first, but as Ron keeps getting louder and more challenging, Peter's responses gets stronger. Finally, the words come out in a yell of revolt. "No, I won't! You go to *your* fuckin' room and *you* stay there!" He is sitting straight, breathing deep and his jaw is set grimly.

After a moment's silence, Ron switches to a normal tone and asks him to tell them what he is angry about, and now Peter can answer directly: "Because she was cold and hard and she scared me."

"Yes," Ron says, "your little boy was scared because she was cruel to you. And you didn't dare move without her permission. That's why you are so tense and wary all the time, even now."

At this point Brad suddenly announces, "You know, I'm a pacifist, and that yelling really shakes me up. I just can't feel that any kind of violence is okay."

"And who was violent in your home?" Kathy's simple question changes Brad's line of thought. Brad replies slowly.

"My Dad and my older brother, I guess. By the time I was in my teens, they were always yelling and cursing and threatening each other. Sometimes it actually came to blows. I hated it."

"That's really hard on a kid. I can see why you'd want to think of yourself as a pacifist," Kathy says, "but if your Dad and your brother were violent, you have that possibility in you, too. What do you do with your violence?"

Brad considers for a moment and then acknowledges half humorously, "I guess I sometimes drive my car pretty violently. You know—like cutting people off if they've done it to me. And I curse at some of the jackasses on the road, under my breath." After a burst of laughing recognition from the class, he continues more thoughtfully, "So I'm misplacing my violence. Maybe it is healthier to get it out here."

Kathy nods and adds, "And you might look at all the other ways you are secretly violent toward yourself and other people, like your son, with all your hostile criticisms and judgments. If you can't cop to your own violence, you bury it inside you and we all get it sooner or later."

Ron reminds them that they need to treat what they do in the next week's anger work sessions with an enormous amount of respect, for they literally will be battling for their lives. "Next week is your chance to make radical shift in how you live your lives. If you don't decide to do something new, then you will go back and do what you always did. Larry will go back and keep on beating himself, and Cheryl will go back and keep on feeling sorry for herself. But it doesn't have to be that way. This is the time when you need to honor the warrior in you. You need to say 'no' to your mother and 'yes' to yourself and mean it."

Anger work at mother

The group arrives for the first experiential anger work session, during which they will express their anger at their mothers fully and openly. They are carrying large sturdy pillows and armed with plastic bats. To begin the session, Ron tells them, "Your power lies in how real you can make this for yourself. If you want to, you can see the image of your mothers in front of you right there on your pillow, and you can fight back with your whole body and all your strength until, this time, you are the one who wins.

"Please understand clearly, you are not here to attack your mother as she is. You are attacking only the negative image you have of her. You are attacking the part of your mother that wasn't aware of your needs or didn't really care when you were a child.

"When your mother was giving you dirty looks, or telling you to get out of her way, or drinking herself to oblivion in the kitchen, you got the message over and over again that you don't matter. So you can't just go up to her now and say, 'Listen to me, mother. I am important, I do matter.' You wouldn't dare say that, and she wouldn't hear you if you did. So the child within you still thinks no one is going to take you and your needs seriously. That is why you are going to have to make her take you seriously."

Ron's voice and manner get more and more forceful. His next

words ring out emphatically. "And, remember, you are doing this work for yourself, not to please the teachers, or to keep up with what anyone else is doing. Let yourself feel what's really coming from inside you. Are you going to stay in her clutches the rest of your life? Is she going to win, or are you? Now, go!"

The thunder of bats striking the big pillows fills the air.

Remarkable things happen when a person confronts the image of mother or father on a large ordinary-looking pillow lying on the floor in front of them. Charlie, angry now at his mother, snatches up his bat and starts furiously whaling away at the pillow. Dorothea knows, though, that his actions are mostly bravado. She stops him after a few minutes and asks him to speak directly to his mother, and tell her firmly that he intends to free himself from her negative influence.

After a moment of silence, the powerful shoulders begin to sag. "Ma," he says in a tentative voice, "I'm going to free myself." He sounds so unsure of himself that Dorothea softly adds the implied words, "If it's all right with you."

Charlie grins uncertainly and shifts his weight. "No, I'm going to do it even if it is not all right with her."

"Okay, tell her so; make her believe it."

He tries again and again. Each time, his voice betrays him by making the statement sound like an appeal. Finally, Dorothea points out that he has a right to be angry at the mother who made him believe that he still has to have her permission before he can act. Now he is in touch with a level of outrage that is entirely different from his earlier display of muscle power, and the work of actually freeing himself is able to begin.

The members rage and swear; sometimes they cry. In one corner, Judy is almost whimpering "Why didn't you love me?" as her bat hits the pillow before her so hesitatingly that it seems more like a pat than a blow. Next to her, Ann stands and swings from her toes, her pleasant young face contorted with rage, soundless except for a slight harsh and triumphant grunt as each blow thuds down.

Marion takes up a position alongside Margie, who hardly notices at first, so focused is she on carrying out the assignment.

"Okay if I play your mother?" Marion calls to her above the din. She nods, determinedly plying the bat, stolidly repeating her catch phrase, "Out of me, get out of me!"

Marion speaks in a a strong, sneering voice. "No way, I'm here to stay. You'll never get away from me!"

Margie bangs harder, but with little more conviction. "No, no! I'm going to get free of you!"

Marion yells louder. "How dare you talk to me like that! I'm your mother and you're supposed to obey me, and you'll do as I say, you hear. For the rest of your life you'll be exactly what I want you to be!"

A little stronger blow. "No, I won't! I'm sixty-six years old. I've finally got to start living my own life before it's too late!"

Now it is clear where the immediate pain is and Marion continues in the role of mother. "Sixty-six years old, seventy-six, eighty-six—you'll go to your grave just the way I taught you to be—a timid little nothing, scared of me, scared of the whole world!"

Bat raised, Margie pauses and looks at Marion and her wavering blue eyes suddenly focus with rage. "No," she whispers, "no." Then her whole body steadies and the whisper becomes a scream. "No, I won't! You're done, do you hear! I'm through with you!" The blows are real now. "If you think I'm going to be scared for the rest of my life because of you . . ."

Marion watches her for another moment to make certain she can maintain her momentum and then tells her exultantly, "Good for you, get her!" before leaving her. In that moment something very important happened in Margie's ability to love herself and eventually to love the memory of her mother.

The members work for the entire evening, pounding the pillows, yelling, cursing, finding where their limits are, backing off and trying again. The noise and excitement in the room is tremendous. The teachers help when necessary, but more and more as the evening goes on they leave the class members to deal with their mothers on their own. By the end of the first evening, some of the members are already feeling triumphant. Some have only inched ahead, but are grimly determined to break free. They all are amazed at the depth and power of the rage they find in themselves.

When the group gathers the next evening for the second session of anger work, Dorothea opens by asking them, "What happened after you left here last night? How did your mother's voice get back into your mind and into your judgments and into your thoughts? What messages did you start listening to again?"

Larry says, "When I was raging last night I felt so clear and powerful. I've never expressed such rage. And during the breaks—I was laying there all sprawled out, stinking with sweat, and I've never felt more alive or real in my entire life. It was wonderful. But as soon as we stopped working and got ready to go home I slipped back into confusion and panic and all that. I heard my mother's voice saying that it really hadn't been that bad when I was a kid, and I should feel guilty for thinking it was. I'm so sick of that kind of guilt!

"But what's different is what happened on the ride home. I could realize that those were her ideas instead of mine. And then I started feeling good. By the time I got home, I actually felt my body and my muscles and I told myself, you did damn good, Larry, and I was really happy with myself. I felt very present in a way I hardly remember feeling before."

Diane says, "I felt really good and powerful last night after we left. I kept catching myself hearing things that she had told me. A memory of her putting me down would pop into my head, and this time I'd yell back at her all the things that I always wanted to say. That felt really powerful. And all night long I kept waking up and hugging myself, and I felt great all day today. But then when I started to get ready to come tonight I suddenly thought, this is just too hard, I can't do it. And I realized that it was her voice coming in again, so now I'm ready to fight back. I want to keep feeling good about myself, and she's not going to take it away from me like she's done all my life!"

During the next anger work sessions, the sense of victory and freedom and selfhood grow more solid for each of the group members. A couple of weeks after decimating the negative image of her mother Kathleen wrote:

> *Once she was out of the way I experienced some fantastic interactions and connections with other people in my class. I have grown to love and care for them in a way which is*

amazing. Then later so many pieces of the puzzle came together for me—that she had such a lonely, barren childhood herself that she really had no chance to be any other way with me. I felt great sadness and love for her, and a sense of how lucky I am to have had a chance to change my life. I am liking myself and liking being with myself more than I ever thought possible. I am learning to love myself and to respect myself in my relationships with other people, and I think that I'll be able to do that with my mother, too, pretty soon. It feels great.

Chapter Five Exercises

Ask yourself these questions and note the answers in your journal or put them on tape.

Exercise 1

a. What did you learn about anger from your mother's way of handling it when you were a child? Did she falsify her anger, releasing it at someone else than the person with whom she was really angry? Did she repress her anger, letting it leak out in indirect ways? Did she act as if there was no such thing?

b. How do you handle your anger today? Are you able to acknowledge anger in a clear, non-blaming way? Can you see a connection between what you usually do now and what you learned from her?

Exercise 2

a. Write out at least half a dozen more scenes from your childhood where you saw your mother acting out her negative traits and giving you negative messages, either verbally or silently.

b. Describe what you were learning about yourself and the world in each of those scenes, and how the beliefs, feelings and behavior you learned are affecting your life today.

c. Look again at the list of mother's negative traits and messages you made in Chapter Four, Exercise 2. How many more of her negative traits are you acting out today, and how many more of her negative messages are you still obeying? Consider each trait and message separately.

Exercise 3

a. Working in a place where you won't be disturbed, imagine that your mother has split into two persons, all that is good and positive about her in one and all that was painful and destructive to you in the other. Let the positive one leave the room, so that you are free to deal with the negative one.

Remember that you are not dealing with your actual

mother of today, but with the negative images you carry in your head of the mother of your childhood. Even if your mother of today still acts out the destructive behaviors you are working with, it is the mother of your childhood you are confronting now.

Before you do the rest of this exercise, be sure that you make contact with your inner guidance for support. Once again, if you find yourself becoming unduly anxious, stop the exercises or continue them with the help of a qualified therapist.

b. Pick one of your emotionally charged negative scenes with your mother. Imagine that you are going to confront your mother in that scene and really speak up for your child. Affirm your right to your anger. If guilty, fearful thoughts about what you are doing come up, ask your guiding spirit to reassure your child that anger is natural and won't hurt anyone when done in imagery. If you find that you are afraid of mother, let your guiding spirit make it safe for you to speak up. (If mother was physically or sexually abusive you may need extra protection: try imagining that you are the director of a play or a TV episode and see the scene from that perspective.)

Write out an impassioned, up-in-arms accusation of her destructive behavior. Tell her what you learned from her in that scene, and how much that has cost you. Come from the perspective of a powerful, indignant advocate for your child. If you actually did fight back when you were a child, see how different it is to speak with real power, not the pretend power of a child. Make your words as vivid as possible. Imagine that someone you trust is urging you on, telling you it's okay to be tough, to be honest, even to be mean, in order to get your point across.

c. Now practice saying the speech aloud. Listen to your voice. If you don't sound strong and angry and sure of yourself (and you may have to try it many times before you do), keep at it until you can hear the determination in your voice and know that you are really standing up for your child.

d. When you have fully expressed your righteous anger about her attitudes and behavior in that scene, notice how you are feeling. There may be bodily relaxation or tingling, emotional excitement or pleasure. Let yourself own and enjoy your positive reactions to having empowered yourself.

This is, of course, only one scene out of many. The goal here is to experiment with what it might be like for you to free yourself from even a small part of your negative mother's domination of your life.

Chapter Six: Confronting Father

Like father, like child

After they complete their anger work at the negative images of their mothers, the members of the group turn to confront their fathers. At the next meeting, Ron asks them to walk around the room silently, imitating how their fathers moved physically and the attitudes their fathers displayed in their postures. "Think about him," he tells the group. "See him as he was while you were growing up. Get the feeling-tone and flavor of how he acted and how he carried his body. Now, imagine that you are stepping into his body and becoming him."

"Feel his attitude toward everything, particularly toward other people. Exaggerate it a little, so it's clear. Now walk around acting out his attitude. As you get a sense of how he was when you were a child, you will get a sense of some of the ways you are now, of the patterns you need to free yourself from."

Following his instructions, the members of the group move around among each other, some aggressively, with chests thrust out, some peering at the others ingratiatingly. A number of them move to the edges of the group, studiously ignoring everyone else.

After they have time to feel in their bodies what their fathers were like, Ron asks them to kneel on the floor. He tells them to imagine that they have become their child selves, and that their fathers are way up above them, physically much bigger. "Now let yourself remember

83

how you had to be in his presence. Did you have to go dead, to hide, to be afraid, or to be his good little girl or his little soldier? Be the person your father trained you to be. Get a sense of how real that feels. How much of your life do you still spend doing that—being someone's obedient little child, or fearful little child, or engaging little child, or someone's rebellious little child?"

Ron then plays father, stepping up close to each of the group members, gazing down at them silently and expressionlessly for a long moment. After he has looked at everyone in turn, he asks them to get up and share any strong feelings they had while he was staring at them. There are very different reactions.

Alicia says, "A lot of fear came up, but I felt angry, too."

"How did you handle the fear and anger?"

"I tried to figure out what you wanted me to do, so I could go ahead and do it, but I hated you all the time."

Ann says. "I had a hard time taking you seriously. I just wanted to say, 'Come on, Dad,' I had a mixture of feeling humiliated and adoring toward you—and making that connection in a sexual way. That's how I feel about my father."

Clearly still in touch with his rage, Arnold says, "When you were looking at me I felt like I wanted to get my fist right in your gut, so you'd really feel it. It's the way I've felt all my life about that fucker. He always had the upper hand because he was bigger and stronger. I remember as a kid trying to project hatred so he could feel it. I couldn't act it out and I couldn't say it, but I could make it come out of my eyes at him. I wanted to let him know that I would do what he said, but I hated him and I had no respect for him."

Ron tells him, "That might be what you needed to do to protect yourself at that time. The problem is that you are still acting that way—still being defiant to anyone you think has power over you—when it's not needed any more. This business of seeing the whole world as full of attacking sons-of-bitches that are out to get you is important for you to explore."

Mike admits, "It was pretty intellectual. I just didn't have any feelings."

Marion suggests, "Maybe you had some feelings and you didn't want to look at them. How did you feel when Ron was looking down at the others?"

"Well, yes," he concedes. "I wanted somebody to nail him. Actually, when Ron stepped up to me I did feel intruded on. But I don't really remember being dominated by my father."

Ron points out, "But the very nature of your relationship with your father is that you are dominated by him. He is big and you are little."

Margie says, "I was so anxious and frightened that my heart still hasn't slowed down. My father didn't physically punish me, but he made me sit on the back porch for hours and think about what I'd done. And I never knew how long it would be before he was going to come and rant on and on about what a bad girl I was and how I disappointed him, till I just felt rotten. As I got older, I'd sit there waiting for him and think angry thoughts, but when I was little I was so scared I didn't know what to do. And as soon as you left I wanted to cry, like I was crumbling from the pressure of it."

Lily says, "When you came over I was ready to do whatever you wanted, just so you would pay some attention to me."

Ron tells her, "So you can see why you let men treat you any way they want. You are so grateful for his attention that you don't even have any filtering system for what kind of attention. Any kind will do."

At the end, Ron tells them all, "Can you see that whatever you do when you act out your relationship with your father is one of your basic attitudes towards life? Out of your fear, out of your longing, out of your emptiness, you adopted ways of protecting yourselves when you were children. But those ways may be destroying you now. To be overcompliant, or fearful, or stubborn may feel comfortable and familiar, but it sabotages you as an adult."

Negative childhood scenes with father

As they continue to write and talk about the negative times with their father in their childhoods, the members of the group begin to reexperience even more strongly the anxiety they felt around him as children.

In a scene that happened when she was about four, which she ironically entitled "Christmas Cheer," Elaine wrote:

> *Daddy is bringing home a Christmas tree and Mom has the door open, and he is cursing 'cause the tree is dropping needles all over the rug and she will ask him to sweep it up. He complains and bitches so much that my mother totally turns him off and ignores him. I can't ignore Daddy that way 'cause he always finds some reason to yell at me and his voice is hard and sharp and he scares me. But then he goes and has a drink and settles down and starts to laugh and is happy not to be working, just drinking.*
>
> *Pretty soon his eyes light up and he gets that bullying, teasing, playful look. He chases me around the house and that is sort of fun and exciting but he is too rough, and pretty soon I'm crying because he is scary and he hurts me. Mom gets angry at both of us because we are making so much noise. After a while, he passes out on the sofa, though, and Mom and I finish decorating the tree. It isn't much fun.*

Considering the effect this scene and others like it with her father had on her adult life, Elaine continued:

> *I never feel good about Christmas or other holidays and festivities. I'm always irritable and grouchy for no apparent reason and I am sure something is going to go wrong. I have another tendency that drives me crazy. I insist on having my own way and I'm very demanding and intolerant, like he was, but I practically invite people to use me and abuse me, the way he did. I say I won't stand for something, and then I find myself putting up with it.*

Larry wrote of a scene that was repeated often in his childhood:

> *My father is whipping my brother. He makes him pull his pants down and he is hitting his bare butt with the belt he uses. I can see the big red welts coming. I know how much it hurts. He finishes with him and looks at me. "Next," he says.*

I am so frightend. "No, please. I won't do it again. I don't know what I did—tell me what I did!" I am crying and ashamed. My sister is standing next to my father. Her punishment is to watch.

"You know what you've done! You've been fighting. Don't make me get up and get you!" He grabs my wrist and pulls me over. He pulls my pants down and begins to whip me. I begin jumping around and yelling because it hurts so much. He threatens to hit me harder if I'm not still, but I can't, so he hits me harder.

When he finishes he says, "Now you kids all hug each other and say how much you love each other." We are all crying and we just stand there. He raises his belt. "Do what I said!" We put our arms around each other and mumble something. Then I run off to cry by myself. I'm so confused and I hurt terribly. I hate my father so much I wish he would die. I feel guilty.

He described the effect on his life starkly:

Vindictive, punishing anger given away to everyone and everything around me for as long as I can remember.

Facing father in the group session

At the next session, Ron tells the group, "Now we are at another tough part of the process, in which you've got to decide again whether you want your life to be different and what you are willing to do about it. For some of you that means you will have to give up your weakness, your silence, your hostility, and your deadness. What else have you learned so far about your relationship with your father?"

Tom says, "I was goofing around today with one of the guys at work who's real cheerful and relaxed all the time and I said something like, 'You know, you are a special guy.' He smiled and said, 'That's what my father used to tell me, that I was real special.'" Tom's voice becomes shaky. "I never heard anything like that. I think he was real lucky."

Kathy asks, "What did you get from your father?"

Tom laughs grimly. "Very critical glances."

"Why do you say 'very critical glances,' and then laugh as if you thought that was funny?" she asks him.

Tom shrugs and answers briefly, "Because that's about all I got from him."

Kathy says, "So your laugh is to let us know you don't need anything from us, since you learned from him that nobody was going to give you anything."

"I guess that's right," Tom admits.

Ron tells him quietly, "You don't need to keep believing that. There are people right here in this room who are trying to have a relationship with you. Who do you think you are protecting yourself from? It made sense once, but you are still protecting yourself now from what frightened you as a child. Can you can feel how your father set you up for that?"

As Tom nods thoughtfully, Brad says, "My father has always been pretty successful at business, and I've never been any good at it. So I feel ashamed and like I'm a failure."

"He didn't want you to succeed like him," explains Ron, remembering Brad's notes. "And then he belittled you because you didn't."

"There was no defense against him. He criticized and sneered at everything I did. He was always angry and contemptuous because I wasn't up to his standards. He still is."

"Our parents train us how to be and then they are angry at us for being that way," Ron comments. "He trains you to be unsure of yourself and then he accuses you of being a failure. So, what are you going to do about it?"

"I've got to stop him from running my life from inside my head."

Playing out the father Brad describes, Ron's manner and voice become loud and bullying. "You just be careful! Everyone else is just as critical of you as I am. You know you can't do anything well enough to make anyone respect you!"

Brad lifts his head and glares at him. Without warning he raises a clenched fist and roars back furiously, "Everyone's not like you! Get the fuck out of my life!"

Dorothea tells him to take a breath and feel his body.

He seems startled and frightened. "I'm shaking! My heart is pounding!"

"Just let it pound," Dorothea tells him. "Let yourself shake." Ron looks at the class. "I hope you all heard that. Those of you who have deadened yourselves in imitation of your fathers, or in reaction to them, try never to feel anything uncomfortable. So you get scared when you start to feel something—tremors, tears, joy. Was there any room in your childhood for that? To act alive was dangerous business in most of your families.

"And some of you think that you have so much rage inside you that you'll never get it all out. Maybe when your father got enraged he went completely out of control and scared you to death. So you think that if you let yourself get in touch with any real emotions, you'll be as crazy as he was. You need to find out for yourself that those fears are not the truth about you. This work is not about trying to get rid of human emotions; it's about having some freedom in what to do with them!"

Ron tells the class that he hopes they know that he and the other teachers are not trying to be mean to them. But if they don't get a sense of what their attitudes and behavior are costing them, they are stuck with it. They will continue to tell themselves stories about how helpless they are and not do anything about it.

"Some of you," he adds, "would rather stay where you are than take a chance on facing your fear. Ann, what are you going to have to give up to free yourself?"

Ann shakes her head. "I'm going to have to give up thinking that I was special to my father, and that he really gave a damn about me. And I'll have to give up being afraid of my own power and of being who I am. And that is really scary because it's like if he's not there, there isn't anything there. I feel like I'm about eight years old right now."

"Isn't that how you feel most of the time?" Ron asks. "Did you ever consider that maybe your life is being run by a scared eight-year-old?"

Kathy adds, "When you take your father off his pedestal you'll be able to come into your own power. Until then, you are using your power to keep him on his pedestal."

Ann said, "I am trying to take him off his pedestal, but I'm afraid of how much it is going to hurt."

Ron is very firm, "You are right—it is going to hurt. The irony of that is, your life hurts already. That's why you are here doing this work. At least this hurt might free you." Turning to the group, he adds, "But most of you want to let go of him with one hand and grab on with the other. And there is nothing 'bad' about doing that. You needed to hang on when you were a kid. But you still want guarantees, you want it to be safe, you want it to be easy. If he'll give you permission, then you're willing to get angry at him. It just doesn't work that way."

Anger work at father

When it is time for the actual father anger work sessions with pillows and bats, most of the members are ready to go at it with a will.

In the middle of the room, Larry swings a belt so wildly that those on both sides automatically give him extra room. Stripped to the waist, he is screaming, "See how it feels, you bastard, you see how it feels!" as he brings the belt down with a ferocious strength hard to believe his skinny body can produce. All around him, people are attacking the pillows that at that moment have become their negative images of their fathers. The yells and curses and the thunder of the bats are deafening. Marion calls a halt to the din after about forty minutes to find out who is in need of support or assistance.

Alicia acknowledges, "I thought that I was really angry at my father and that I was right on schedule, but tonight I can hardly do anything. I don't seem to have any energy. What do you do when you get stuck like that?"

Kathy tells her, "One thing you can do is be glad that you recognize that you are stuck. I hope all of you sometimes get surprised by how stuck you are. If you think you are doing this work perfectly, then you are probably just doing an act. If you feel like half the time you don't know what you are doing, then you are right on schedule."

"Yes," said Alicia. "I don't want to just hit a pillow and jump around and shout at him. I want something to really change."

"Then you've got to change it!" Marion challenges her. "You've got to make it real. Nobody else can do it for you. When you are facing that pillow, it's just you and your father. You have got to say 'No' to him and mean it. This is your chance to rescue the child inside you who has been angry and afraid and stuck with all the negative traits he modeled for you. No one else can rescue your child, that's your job."

Some people need help from the teachers to focus themselves. Others are clear on what they need to do to confront the negative image of the father they carry inside them, that is, to confront their own fear and anger. They are able to do it with little assistance other than the supportive environment. For everyone, the work is gut-wrenching, at times frightening, and eventually exhilarating.

Angie, slim and elegant even in her jogging clothes, tries to face the image of the father who had abused her sexually from the time she was seven years old till she ran away at fifteen. She breaks into helpless whimpering. She is determined; she knows that her fear and hatred of him interferes with every relationship she has and is even now destroying her recent marriage. But each time she raises her bat, the old terror engulfs her again.

It is not until Dorothea, playing the part of the protective mother she never had, puts one arm around her and starts striking the pillow with another bat, angrily declaring, "Don't you dare touch Angie, you old bastard, or I'll kill you!" that Angie is able to begin to find her own courage.

Later she wrote:

> When Dorothea started to scream at my father, the most incredible feeling happened. For a moment, I couldn't believe that there was anyone who would stand up to him, and I kept remembering how my own mother had never really stopped him, in fact she acted like she didn't want to know what he was doing to me. No one had ever stood up for me.
>
> For the first time, I really got that the teachers, and all my brothers and sisters in the class, were on my side. I could see

that he really didn't have any right to do what he'd done, that he was the one who was bad and evil; it wasn't me. I was just a little kid who wanted him to pay attention to me and love me. Then I finally started to get mad. I beat on him and beat on him and I felt like I never wanted to stop.

She does stop, though not till after she has "beat on him" many times. In the experience of destroying him and his power over her, she feels the fullness of victory and of her own strength. Only a few weeks later she will be able to free herself further by experiencing a level of compassion and understanding she never imagined possible for this man who had terrorized her all through her childhood.

Chapter Six Exercises

Note: The first three exercises in this chapter repeat for your father the work you did in Chapter Five for your mother.

Ask yourself these questions and note the answers in your journal or put them on tape.

Exercise 1

a. What did you learn about anger from your father's way of handling it when you were a child? Did he falsify his anger, releasing it at someone other than the person with whom he was really angry? Did he repress his anger, letting it leak out in indirect ways? Did he act as if there was no such thing as anger?

b. Can you see a connection between how you handle your anger today and what you learned from him?

Exercise 2

a. Write out at least half a dozen more scenes from your childhood where you saw your father acting out his negative traits and giving you negative messages, either verbally or silently.

b. Describe what you were learning about yourself and the world in each of those scenes, and how those beliefs, feelings and behavior are affecting your life today.

c. Look again at the list of father's negative traits and messages you made in Chapter Four, Exercise 2. How many more of his negative traits are you acting out today, and how many more of his negative messages are you still obeying? Consider each trait and message separately.

Exercise 3

a. Working in a place where you won't be disturbed, imagine that your father has split into two persons, all that is good and positive about him in one and all that was painful and destructive to you in the other. Let the positive one leave the room, so that you are free to deal with the negative one.

Remember that you are not dealing with your actual father of today, but with the negative images you carry in your head of the father of your childhood. Even if your father of today still acts out the destructive behaviors you are working with, it is the father of your childhood you are confronting now.

Before you do the rest of this exercise, be sure that you make contact with your inner guidance for support. Once again, if you find yourself becoming unduly anxious, stop the exercises or continue them with the help of a qualified therapist.

b. Pick one of your emotionally charged negative scenes with your father. Imagine that you are going to confront your father in that scene and really speak up for your child. Affirm your right to your anger. If guilty, fearful thoughts about what you are doing come up, ask your guiding spirit to reassure your child that anger is natural and won't hurt anyone when done in imagery. If you find that you are afraid of father, let your guiding spirit make it safe for you to speak up. (If father was physically or sexually abusive you may need extra protection: try imagining that you are the director of a play or a TV episode and see the scene from that perspective.)

Write out an impassioned, up-in-arms accusation of his destructive behavior. Tell him what you learned from him in that scene, and how much that has cost you. Come from the perspective of a powerful, indignant advocate for your child. Make your words as vivid as possible.

c. Now practice saying the speech aloud. Listen to your voice. If you don't sound strong and angry and sure of yourself (and you may have to try it many times before you do), keep at it until you can hear the determination in your voice and know that you are really standing up for your child.

d. When you have fully expressed your righteous anger about his attitudes and behavior in that scene, notice how you are feeling. There may be bodily relaxation or tingling, emotional excitement or pleasure. Let yourself own and enjoy your positive reactions to having empowered yourself.

This is, of course, only one scene out of many. The goal here is to experiment with what it might be like for you to free yourself from even a small part of your negative father's domination of your life.

Exercise 4

a. Imagine your grownup self returning to the home of your childhood. See yourself letting yourself in through the front door and searching through the house until you find your small self who was so unhappy and unseen in that household. Greet your child (who knows you at once) gently and tenderly. Pick up your small self and take her or him away with you from the negativity in that house.

b. Take a pillow or a stuffed animal in your arms, imagining that it is your inner child when very young. Say to your child the words you must have longed to hear from your mother and father. Try, "you are perfect just as you are," "I love you so much," "I'm so glad you're mine." Make up other phrases that feel right to you. Can you sense your inner child's response?

Stage III: Forgiveness

Chapter Seven: Growing Past Anger

Validating Progress

A marked change from the heaviness and nervous anxiety of the previous weeks is apparent as the group comes in to the next session after their anger work. Even though they have completed only part of the Process, definite shifts in attitude are obvious. There is animated talk and ease between the members, and they greet the teachers with something approaching camaraderie. They are feeling a new kind of connectedness with everyone who went through the wars with them, and a new sense of their own presence and power.

"What have you learned about yourself?" asks Ron. It is crucial at this point that the members of the group notice each positive new development and acknowledge it. This solidifies the changes that have already occurred, and encourages them to expect many more positive changes to come.

Have they been able to validate what they have achieved? It is one thing to stand up to your parents in the excitement of shared accomplishment with teachers and fellow group members. It is another thing to stay with your victory and strength later when you are on your own at home or at work.

Judy says cheerfully, "I'm feeling pretty feisty, with a lot more energy. I've been a lot more assertive this week, too, and a lot freer."

Others in the group talk about how they are learning to claim their right to do things in their own way, and how good that feels, though so different as to seem almost unnatural. They also speak of beginning to recognize more of their negative patterns, such as constantly comparing themselves with others, or not paying attention to what they are doing, without criticizing or judging themselves harshly.

Mike says, "I sent my mother some flowers for her birthday and she called me. After she thanked me, she started complaining about my youngest brother not remembering her birthday, and got into her usual self-pity routine. I started to slip back into the same old pattern of feeling guilty, like I should have reminded him or something, and then resenting her. But I caught myself and stayed pretty centered and objective. I was able to just listen and tell her I was sorry she was feeling sad. So I'm feeling some freedom from her clutches and more self-empowered."

Marion congratulates him. "When you catch a pattern like that, you are already ahead of most of the human race. Most people think they are only reacting to what is happening out there. They don't realize that they are mainly on automatic, repeating something they've done a thousand times before."

She adds that if they are willing to change their beliefs about themselves, if they are willing to "grow up" in the best sense of that phrase and take control of their own lives, all of them might actually have a real relationship with their parents. Then they will be capable of extending the possibility of a relationship to anybody.

Charlie sounds less happy. "I feel very empty after the anger work. It's like all of a sudden I have a lot of room, but I don't know how to fill it up. I don't know how to make things different." He looks at Ron expectantly.

Ron nods, "When you gain your freedom from the images of your mother and father, there is often a sense of emptiness—they took up a lot of space. What if you gave yourself time to see what you create out of that emptiness, rather than trying to find another roadmap about how your life is supposed to be? Freedom means that you can move around, not that you exchange a little prison for a bigger one."

"I had such a hard time expressing my anger at my parents," Peter says. "But now I feel that nothing can be taken away from me. I can go through my fear, and then I feel solid."

Dorothea agrees, "When you allowed yourself to experience the things you were afraid of, you found you had the strength within you to deal with it. Now you know you have that strength."

Diane is exhilarated. She says, "I felt so much more centered this week, even in arguing with my husband. I usually pull back and go into my silent anger numbers when I don't like what he is doing. This week I realized that I don't have to be absolutely sure I am right and the other person is wrong before I can express myself. I still am kind of afraid of expressing myself openly, but I decided that it's okay to be a little bit afraid, and go ahead and do it anyway."

"Yeah," says Ron. "In the past, being afraid has meant 'I stop, I go numb, I run away.' Now you can say, 'I know that I'm afraid, and now what do I want to do?' It means you can keep exploring. Everything that's scary can become liberating if you change your mind about it."

She nodded. "My husband sure does things that push my buttons, though."

"Actually, the people who push our buttons most can be our best teachers—they can show us where we are not finished with our own work." Ron shakes his head, looking amused. "I hate knowing that. Because it means that all the jerks who show up in my life are there to teach me something. God, I hate having to admit that!

"Remember, this work is about how we are being, not how we want someone else to be. It's not, 'I will be honest and loving if she will, or if she will at least be impressed when I'm honest and loving.' We may prefer to choose the company of people who support us, but if we can't be how we want to be, regardless of how other people are being, we will keep on feeling disappointed and resentful."

He goes on to point out that, if we don't welcome the people who push our buttons as an opportunity to learn about ourselves, we are stuck with the belief that our lives would be fine if only they would straighten up. There is an enormous trap in that, because it means that we've decided that we can't live our lives the way we want until someone else changes.

Ann says, with a bit of self-mockery that draws friendly laughter from the class, "This week my boyfriend did all the things I've been afraid he was going to do—like leave me." She chokes up a little and then adds firmly, "It isn't so bad though, because I'm learning that I can live through it, and I never thought I could. I am looking at it as a really big challenge, but it's awfully painful."

"There are painful things in life," Ron agrees. "Our choice is to feel them and work with them or just to react automatically. To stay with what is true in the pain is the way you can learn more about yourself and your capacities and your own integrity. Sometimes it doesn't mean that the pain is any less. But the story you tell yourself about the pain changes."

He goes on to encourage her to honor the fact that this is a difficult time for her and allow herself to feel it, without feeling sorry for herself and without numbing out. "If we lose somebody, we need to let ourselves feel our sadness, and permit ourselves to mourn. If we're not deeply touched when someone leaves us or dies, it means that we haven't let them in very far."

Ann agrees, "Somehow, even the quality of the pain is better. The sadness I felt about Jason's leaving was really deep and true instead of self-pity. I cried for a long time, but I didn't feel destroyed."

Kathleen strikes a different note, "I've been afraid these past couple of days. Since I separated myself from my mother and father I've been more in touch with fear and loneliness than I have with hope and strength."

Ron nods. "You've worked hard to separate yourself from your childhood images of your parents and all the limiting beliefs you learned from them, and many of you probably are kind of tender and naked right now. If you have the courage to simply accept that you are scared and that you do feel alone, you'll begin to feel your own power. Then you can begin to learn how to nurture yourself.

"The other thing is, if you aren't willing to let yourself experience being alone, you can't ever have close relationships. That's because the child in you believes, 'If I get close to somebody they might leave, and then I would feel lonely and that would kill me.' So until you find out that you can live through loneliness, you'll never let anyone get too close—even though you may think you want that more than anything. When you know that you can handle whatever might happen, relationships stop feeling so dangerous."

Larry says, "I was really afraid to make decisions, because I felt that every decision I made was irreversible. I'm beginning to find out that's really not true. I have the right to make a decision and then change my mind. It is just me deciding, and I'm responsible to myself. There is a lot of freedom in that."

Ron validates his statement and adds that just because our parents told us that we were never supposed to make mistakes doesn't mean that it is true. Most people out there aren't waiting to get us. Most people have made mistakes and it won't amaze them too much if we also make mistakes.

"Do you realize that if we'd been afraid to make mistakes when we were a year old we would never have learned to walk? Babies learn to walk because they don't have anyone telling them that they are being very ungraceful and the neighbors are watching. Babies want to walk so bad that they may fall down a hundred times, but they'll learn to walk. They don't think, 'Hey, I tried twice, and it hurt when I fell down. I'm just not cut out for this kind of thing.' We would still be crawling, with the amount of time some of us give ourselves to keep trying something new."

Margie says, "At first, I felt really good about separating from my parents and getting clearer about who I am. But on Friday I started feeling depressed again, and it seemed so familiar. I felt like I could just stay that way, it wasn't too bad. But then I remembered my mother's endless depressions, and realized that I have a choice now about letting myself be that way or not. I just decided I don't have to do that. That felt really good."

"That's exactly what I experienced this week!" Tom breaks in excitedly. "I don't have to carry on with obsessive thoughts about being scared. I can just recognize what I'm doing. The sooner I stop obsessing about being scared, and just let go of it, the sooner I can shift into another mode. I've had experiences this week of shifting back and forth, and I've actually enjoyed it."

101

"Yeah," says Ron, "I've discovered that I tend to have certain kinds of reactions whenever I feel threatened. What's important is knowing that, not trying to fix it so that I never feel threatened again. I think the only way any of us could live our lives without feeling threatened occasionally is by never getting out of bed. But I can watch what I do and notice that under certain conditions I tend to react in certain ways. Then I can decide how I want to handle it this time. In learning to know ourselves and recognize the stories we tell ourselves we can begin to have some choice in our lives."

"What, are you saying that you are still not perfect, Ron?" demands Charlie playfully. "You mean we never get finished?"

Ron picks up the challenge. "Why would you want to be finished with learning to know more and more about your feelings and your truth and who you are?"

Arnold joins the teasing. "So we'd have weekends to do something else besides homework?" The class bursts into laughter. Almost all of them have complained, sometimes bitterly, about the the amount of homework they have been given.

Ron shares the amusement and then answers seriously. "At least your weekends can be yours from now on, instead of belonging to your parents." He adds, "The temptation we all have is to finish a piece of work and think that we don't have to pay attention to what we learned anymore. It's as if we thought that learning to be truthful and aware and to make our own choices is some sort of homework assignment. The payoff is not that you get an 'A' at the end of this course, but that you get your own life back."

Cheryl says, "For the first time in my life, I feel as if I am comprehending things in my classes in college, because my emotional reactions aren't taking up all my attention. I still have to go over things a lot, but I feel like I'm making connections much easier."

Alicia says, "I've been looking for something out there all my life, and I'm finally beginning to believe that it's in here, not out there. It's an incredible shift."

Judy brings up another, urgent question. "Is this going to go away? I mean, these last weeks were so profound. Is the way that we're feeling now going to last? I worry about that."

Ron knows she is strong enough now to be challenged. "The amount of freedom you are feeling now is not an accident, Judy. You made some choices that got you there. So you don't have to just wonder what is going to happen next week. What do you want to happen next week? Are you willing to pay attention and be there for yourself? Are you willing to take time to learn what nourishes you? Or are you going to go back to your automatic childhood programs? You will choose either consciously or unconsciously how you'll be next week, but you will make a choice."

He adds that holding on to what we are feeling is as much of a mistake as not feeling anything. If we can accept that the nature of feelings is that they move through us, then everything we feel can be fresh and new all the time. If we try to hold on to what we are feeling in one situation, the feelings appropriate to another time and another situation cannot arise.

After the group members take a moment to digest this, Brad speaks up, "I feel that I've begun to make some progress with the shitty relationship I've had with my fourteen-year-old son. He's coming back very slowly and tentatively. I told him what I'm learning in this class, but I don't think he really understands, or that he's quite ready to see Daddy with different eyes. But I can see the beginning of a change, though we've got a long way to go."

Ron grins. "That's lucky. Since we've got a long way to go, we don't have to be perfect from the start, do we? This is the time to just jump in and experiment with making the changes you want."

Changing our imagery

Once we have been able to separate ourselves from our childhood images of mother and father, and we have become aware without judgment of the negative patterns we are still living out, we can consciously experiment with new behavior. We can affect our ongoing experience by deliberately changing the negative childhood images that ordinarily guide our thoughts and behavior.

Experiments have shown that the connection between our imagery and how we feel and act is strong. When electrodes are attached to the legs of a person who is standing perfectly still while picturing the act of running, the nerves of the running muscles will fire off. In another experiment, the members of a basketball team regularly imaged themselves as practicing. They improved their game as much as the comparison team that actually was practicing. Imagery is not just fantasy; it is a power that is real and available to us. Our imagery molds the reality we experience.

At this point, the members of the group are shown a simple way to change the imagery that is holding their negative patterns in place. Marion asks them to close their eyes and leads them through the imagery step by step.

First, remember something you have done recently that is a repetition of one of the patterns you've decided you don't want to continue. For example, it might be the pattern of constantly comparing yourself with others.

Second, remember which one of your parents you learned that pattern from, to remind yourself that it is only learned behavior, not an intrinsic part of you. Remember how they learned it from their parents in turn.

Third, make a careful inner search for the most fitting word or phrase for the negative attitude or behavior you saw yourself demonstrating. In the example, the phrase might be "seeing myself as one down," or simply "always comparing."

Fourth, see your guiding spirit removing that word or phrase from inside of you, and replacing with a new and healing word or phrase, the opposite of the original. If you leave the choice of the constructive new idea entirely to your guiding spirit (instead letting your intellect figure it out), there will be a sense of surprise and relief about how precisely it provides the needed antidote.

After you have given yourself time to sense the pleasurable feelings connected with the new term your guiding spirit has given you, the final step is to imagine yourself reliving the original problem situation, this time with the new attitude or feeling you have been given.

Alicia described one of her re-imagings like this:

> *Situation: Maria and Josie [her younger sisters] tell me that they are going to vacation together in Mexico this year. They don't even ask me if I want to go. I feel left out, even though*

we all know I don't have the free time to go. I think about how close they have gotten to each other in the past couple of years. I feel that I have been discarded, and I'm hurt and resentful.

Name for the pattern: Jealousy and possessiveness.

Tracing the pattern to my mother: My mother was possessive of all of us. I remember her getting upset if she thought my father or my sisters and I were up to something and weren't including her. She would get her feelings hurt, and be jealous and resentful.

Re-imaging: The words jealous/possessive are a dull, dark green and have something like a tangle of roots holding them together. My spirit replaces those words with the letters for the word "loved," made out of beautiful pink camellias. I take in the fragrance and beauty of the camellias, and let myself feel loved.

Reenacting the scene in imagery while feeling loved: My sisters come in the room and tell me about their trip. I am glad for them and want to hear all about it. I tell them frankly that I wish I could go, too. They hug me and say they feel really good about my wanting to be with them, and we make plans to get together after they return. I feel light and happy.

"As simple as the imagery for healing your patterns may seem," Ron tells them, "there are requirements for doing it effectively. You have to have enough courage to look at your own attitudes and behavior and recognize that there is something you want to change. Then, you have to have the patience to trace the pattern back to your childhood and see where you learned it. In other words, first you have to own the pattern, and then you have to recognize that it's not really you, it's just how you were taught to behave. Then you have to be willing to let go of it and to use your imagery to allow another possibility to emerge."

As situations occur in our lives, the connections in our minds ordinarily switch back to the image we have of the last time something similar happened to us, and we automatically react as we've done in the past. There are parts of our minds, however, that don't seem to know the difference between imagery and reality, so re-imaging actually creates new responses. Once we have loosened our dependency on mother and father, however, we can re-image the situation in a positive way and give ourselves a new experience. The next time a similar situation happens to us, our minds switch back to the imagery experience and find the new pattern to copy. Re-imaging is not denial, it is admitting what is really happening, and then permitting our own inner wisdom to offer us an alternative.

"Furthermore," Ron continues, "when you do this kind of re-imaging, you will come to know yourself better. For instance, you may find that there are some patterns you are not willing to heal. You may find yourself thinking 'He acted like a jerk. I'm angry and I don't intend to let it go.' You might even find out that you don't want to let anything go, and then you can begin investigating that. Perhaps you have a pattern of holding on to grudges because your mother or your father did, and you need to deal with that before you can do much with the other one."

Mike has some difficulty in learning this method of changing his reactions. He goes through the steps of trying to re-image his continuing tendency to feel arrogant and superior to other people, noting how his father and mother had both behaved as if they were infinitely superior to people with less education or status. He thinks the new term ought to be "compassion," but isn't sure his guiding spirit is providing it.

His notes read:

> *I sense my intellect is working a lot on the positive opposite part of the re-imaging and not leaving it up to my spirit. I have little trouble letting images for the negative stuff come up (like black cast-iron letters that are so heavy they hurt my hands when I try to grab them), but the image for the positive stuff they are supposed to turn into often eludes me.*

His teacher points out that he needs to deal with the pattern he learned from his father of rejecting the good in life and seeing only what is negative, before he can deal effectively with his remaining tendencies toward superiority and arrogance. Using re-imagery he begins to learn about the freedom he now has to value what is good and worthwhile around him instead of automatically rejecting it.

The results of re-imaging are as varied as the group members themselves. Judy re-images "self-consciousness," expecting to get something about being self-assured. Instead, her guide gives her the words "concern for others," and helps her to realize that her self-consciousness has much to do with her vanity. Ann re-images "fear of public speaking" and gets "sparkling." As she relives one of the talks she has to give in her job, she experiences herself tossing aside the prepared talk and coming to life as she speaks from her own quirky and humorous self. It is something of a revelation, for she had never considered doing that.

"You may have to re-image the same pattern a number of times, because some patterns are deeply engrained." Marion tells them, "but after you have re-imaged it successfully, instead of immediately going into your old reactions when something comes up, you will have new possibilities. 'I can stand up for myself,' or 'I can get centered instead of getting angry.' It is not that there is any one particular way you should behave. If you have more choices, you will be freer."

In letting their guiding spirits offer them alternatives to the reactions that had been automatic since their childhoods, the group members learn to solidify and extend the progress they have already made. This, too, is preparation for the next step, the movement from anger to forgiveness.

Chapter Seven Exercises

Ask yourself these questions and note the answers in your journal or put them on tape.

Exercise 1

    a. Are you aware of anything different in yourself after confronting your mother and father in each of those scenes?

    b. What would your life be like if you were able to let go of your learned automatic reactions and respond to situations openly and spontaneously instead?

Exercise 2

    A re-imaging visualization is given in the second half of this chapter, with examples of how it works.

    a. Think of a recent episode in your life in which you acted out a pattern of behavior that you don't want to continue, and follow each of the five steps given for re-imaging it.

    b. Imagine reliving the problem situation with your new, positive attitude. Do you see a difference in what happens?

Chapter Eight: Compassion and Forgiveness

From anger to compassion

The members of the group have gone through weeks of preparation for the stage of forgiveness. They have recognized, acknowledged, and expressed the full extent of the destructive messages they received as children, and seen how those messages affect their adult lives. They have given the child inside themselves permission to carry out the desire for revenge and self-assertion; to stand up to the images of their parents (who were the perpetrators of this outrage against them) and punish them fully.

The validity and energy of their anger has empowered the members to break their emotional dependence on their parents. They have overcome the fear that they would lose their parents' love and approval, or that their parents could hurt them further. Now they are ready to move on to another kind of energy—the open, healing, holistic energy of compassion. They are ready to discover that they are big enough to let go of further desire for revenge, and to feel empathy and compassion for the mothers and fathers against whom they have been raging. This step will further break the grip of their negative programming, and strengthen the foundations of their freedom and ability to love.

At the beginning of the next session, though, there is some hesitation.

"It feels good to just let myself get mad, now." Brad says. "I've found it makes me feel much more alive than beating up on myself all the time. But I'm scared you people are going to make me drop it and be compassionate."

Tom feels the same way. "First thing that came to me when you said we could understand what happened to our mothers is, 'Shit, my mind has been thinking up reasons why she did this to me for years.' I'm afraid of going back into that, instead of keeping this connection with myself that I've got now."

Ron tells them, "So your working agenda now is to discover the difference between the agony of denying yourself and trying to feel pity for your mother, and the high experience of being yourself and feeling compassion for another human being who was trapped like you have been.

"The idea at this point is not to forgive your mother for being a martyr, but to question, just what would make a woman become a martyr? And the way we'll do this is to explore what happened to her in her childhood—not to deny anything, or to be defensive about what she did, but to understand."

"But I'm not ready to give up being mad at my mother," protests Judy. "I just learned how to do that! I like feeling more powerful than she is." Never before in her life having experienced a real expression of anger, Judy is so thrilled with her new power that she doesn't want to let go of it. She is afraid that she may become weak or scared again. She needs to learn that there is a greater power than anger.

Dorothea replies, "Maybe you'll find out that compassion also makes you feel powerful. The reality is that we need to feel our pain fully in order to acknowledge what is true for us. We need our anger in order to change things. But really to be free to live as we want, we also need love and compassion.

"Some of you may have to do more anger work before you are ready to start the next stage of the work. The crucial question at this point is not whether you are totally through with your anger at your parents, but whether you are still afraid of what your parents can do to you. Anger can overcome fear, but anger is always a way of handling fear. As long as we remain angry, we are still afraid. It is not possible to feel real compassion for someone we fear."

"Compassion is neither pity nor sympathy," Marion tells them, "nor is it weakness or self-effacement. It is the deep recognition of another's pain, with the desire to help. With compassion, you can say to another person, 'I understand your pain because I recognize my own. Out of my pain I have hurt a lot of people, and out of your pain, you have hurt a lot of people. Since I understand that about both of us, I can drop the recriminations and guilt flinging.'"

She continues to lay the groundwork for the next step. "It is true that your parents did the things you have been rightfully enraged at them for," she tells them. "But it is also true that they were not to blame for it. Even while you continue to be aware of the reality of what your child suffered, you can understand that what happened to you also happened to them."

Considering Marion's words, Charlie says thoughtfully, "I've got such a problem with my wife, because I'm enraged at her so much of the time. Maybe if I can understand my mother and have compassion for her, I'll feel better about my wife, too. But my wife does do some things that just tick me off."

Marion says, "We are not asking you to give up your ability to get angry. There undoubtedly will be times in your life when you need it. We are inviting you to explore another capacity that you have. You are more than just an angry person, you know; you are also a tender and loving person. This is your chance to know that part of yourself."

Ann says, "I feel like compassion is such a deep emotion. I don't know how I can possibly feel it deeply enough to change things. I can't imagine myself crying for my parents."

To give her a way to loosen her mindset, Dorothea suggests, "But you can begin to realize that, even though you suffered as a child, you have an opportunity to do something about it. Most of your parents are going to be stuck where they are. They will go to their graves, if they haven't already, doing the same negative kinds of things that they are doing now. You have a chance at a whole new life. They don't."

Ann's notes about this part of the session show how well she understands. She wrote:

> *I know that one thing that holds me up is that I'm afraid my mother will take credit for it if I am at peace, and I don't want to let her take credit for anything positive in my life. But I also*

*know that if I keep that kind of chain around my heart I
won't be able to let anyone else in. I can see how I can be just
as tied to my mother by hating her as by being dependent on
her.*

Dorothea reminds them, "If we stay angry, we must hold on to
pain, fear and resentment to justify our anger, which means that we
continue to live with pain, fear, and resentment. Each time these
feelings arise, our peace of mind is destroyed. It means, too, that we
must live with constant, low-level tension, with our anger always
ready to defend us. It means also that we are likely to transfer our
feelings about our parents to anyone and everyone in our environment."

The group is quietly attentive now. They have all known from the
beginning that the expression of their rage at their parents was only
a step. No matter how estranged they are from their mothers and
fathers, or hopeless about the relationship they have with them—
they really want to be reconciled in some way.

The value of compassion and forgiveness

Forgiveness is the full willingness to respond to someone we
believe has injured us, not with anger and punishment, but with love
and compassion. As we let go of the need for resentment, blaming,
self-justification and revenge, we also are letting go of our programmed
reactions and making space for the essential qualities of love,
generosity, kindness, and compassion. Forgiveness permits us to
access the goodness within ourselves.

The willingness to forgive and be forgiven is entirely different from
emotional dependency. When we are emotionally dependent, we
sacrifice our own nature to try to become what we think our parents
(or other people) want us to be. When we are able to be separate and
to affirm ourselves, we can be in relationship with others and still be
ourselves. Just as we feel our strength and individuality through the
righteous expression of anger, we can feel it even more deeply
through letting go and forgiveness.

We will not be able to forgive ourselves for how we have acted out
of our childhood programming unless we can forgive our parents for

how they acted out of their childhood programming. If we can understand why our parents were the way they were, we finally will be capable of fully understanding why we are the way we are. The truth is that we can never find full understanding and compassion for ourselves, or anyone else, until we have found understanding and compassion for our parents.

If we cannot reach compassion within ourselves, we are caught in believing that the only way to be strong is to be tough and angry. The reality is that the stronger we become, the safer we feel, and the more tender we can become. Then we can begin to discover that, other people's behavior may make us sad, but it doesn't offend us so much anymore. We can permit ourselves to recognize the reality that people often treat each other very badly.

To feel compassion for our parents does not mean that we approve of what they have done, or that it didn't have consequences. It is possible to take the next step toward disentangling ourselves from the whole melodrama, however, by recognizing that even as we began as innocent, vulnerable little children, so did they.

Mother was once a child, too

As with the loss and grief work and the anger work, the forgiveness work with the images of mother and father is separate. First, the members of the group work with the images of their mothers. This time they begin not with the adult mother they yearned for and fought with but with mother as a child—a child at the mercy of her own parents.

Kathy asks the group to settle themselves comfortably in their chairs and take a deep breath as they close their eyes.

Kathleen's notes about the guided visualization that follows said:

> *When my three selves are separated out, it is nice to see that my intellect doesn't look so rigid and disapproving anymore, and my spirit just flows around lighting up the whole scene. My child is about thirteen. She seems very comfortable; she's dressed in jeans and a plaid shirt. My spirit brings in my mother as a child of the same age. She has dark hair and her eyes look big and sad like a Keane picture. I feel a little wary,*

113

though. She always used her sadness to make me feel sorry for her.

My spirit draws any remaining anger and distrust out of me and fills me with curiosity instead. Then she sends honesty and openness, and a desire to share her story with me, into the child of my mother. I find that I want to reach out and touch her hands, to assure her that I really want to understand her.

With the guidance of Kathy's evocative words, the two children sit down together to get acquainted. The child of mother is asked how she had learned to act in one of the particular ways that was so deeply troublesome, and is encouraged to respond. Inevitably the same attitudes and behavior that destroyed the happiness of each person's childhood prove to be a reflection of what happened in their mother's childhood.

After Kathy brings the group members back to the room, she asks what the experience was like for them.

Diane says, "I'm not sure I found out anything particularly new so far. But just seeing her in that context, when we're both children, and so innocent—I found I wanted to ask her to play with me, and I began to cry. I think I started to feel some compassion for her for the first time in my life."

Tom says, "There were things I hadn't noticed before, like how lonely she was and how abusive her mother was to her. It hadn't ever sunk in."

Kathy explains that they will continue at home with this kind of imaged dialogue between the child of their mother and their own child, until they understand how their mother learned all of her major negative patterns.

"The important thing to realize," she says, "is that in many ways your mother was actually a little girl trapped in a woman's body. Most of you can get that sense if you see her as a pained, ignored, tormented child that probably no one ever listened to. It doesn't mean that her behavior to you was justified. It just means that you can understand how she got that way."

She adds that they might come to realize that probably one of their

114

mother's greatest sorrows was that she lost her relationship with them. Because of being stuck in childhood programming, their mothers had driven them away.

"You have an opportunity not to do that in the rest of your life," she says. "You don't have to lose your own children because you are acting out of your childhood programming. You don't have to lose yourself, either. And it will be possible for you to create a new and different relationship with your mother and father."

Most of the group members are ready to move toward under-standing and compassion, though a few of them are still not through with the explosive anger in which they had all been engaged. Larry has been so angry for so long that he simply doesn't feel he had enough time to "get it all out." Ron tells him that he needs to spend more hours raging at his mother, letting his anger take him over again and again, until he recognizes that it flares up mechanically whenever he feels afraid of her.

Arnold, only partly joking, throws in another idea. "But what will I do with myself if I'm not being angry all the time? I'm afraid I'll get bored."

Ron nods. "You know, it's funny, but it's true. Part of the reason we don't to want give up being angry is that we are afraid that we won't know what to do with ourselves. It's like we've built our lives around being upset and frustrated at other people. So now we have to create another model of what it means to be excited and joyful and creative—and committed to ourselves."

The way it really was for mother

In their further imagery work at home the group members take themselves back into the scene they enacted in the session with the child of their mother. They ask their mother's child how she learned each one of the major destructive attitudes and behaviors she passed on to them. Her reply must be personal and detailed, with a scene, if possible, showing what happened. Here the truth of how beliefs, behaviors, and attitudes are passed down from one generation to the next becomes starkly clear. The members find that in her childhood their mother was treated the same way she treated them. If she was filled with self-pity, it turned out that one of her parents had played the martyr. If she was cruel, either her father or mother had been cruel to her.

They are asked not to bring in material their mothers actually had told them earlier about her childhood, since such memories are often idealized. What is needed now is for the members to accept what their own imagery shows them about how she learned to become the mother they knew. The material that comes forth often surprises them.

Lily wrote:

> *My grandmother was always nice to my brothers and sister and me. I couldn't believe it when I saw how mean she was to my mother when she was a little girl. But then I remembered how my Mom still always seems to be nervous when Grandma visits, rushing around trying to please her, and it begins to make sense.*

After all of their mother's most important attitudes and behaviors are understood, the members are told to bring to mind anything about which they are still not satisfied. They are encouraged deliberately to bring up any anger they may still be feeling, and to confront their mothers with any resentments they still have until they are fully resolved.

Sometimes a problem that prevents understanding must be explored in an individual session. In his notes, Brad described such a session with his teacher, Marion:

> *Marion had my mother and me talk some more about how she had learned to treat me the way she had, how her mother had made her feel so bad about herself and criticized her so much and treated her pretty little sister so much better. She told me about how when her sister was born, her mother kept talking about what a beautiful, healthy baby this one was, and then she said, "This is my precious one." Just seeing the hurt way the child of my mother looked when she said that, I began to feel some sorrow for her.*
>
> *Then Marion asked my mother to tell me whether there was anything more she wanted to say to me. And I heard her*

116

say that she felt great pain in her heart to hear what I had gone through, and pain to hear how I felt about her. And she felt such sorrow that she hadn't been able to see my suffering, anymore than her mother had seen hers.

And I just felt the most tremendous longing, because she had never really spoken to me that way. I felt such a sense of loss, and then an acceptance that she never will, except in my imagery. It is so sad that mother and son should have been so far apart, when we are so much alike and could have given each other so much. It is so, so sad for both of us. And then I felt my heart open to her, and I knew I could forgive her, because I know that she would have been different if she could.

Before they complete the group session, Ron talks a little more about the fact that they will never be able to see their parents' plight if they still want them to be their big mommy or big daddy. In that case, they will perpetually be disappointed.

"What you are trying to do is to see your parents as fellow human beings on the same planet," he reminds them. "We might learn how we can stop people from causing so much pain in the world if we could understand what led up to it."

Ann was hesitant. "I'm still a little afraid that if I feel compassion for her, she'll just take over again. It seems like I'm giving up my only defense."

"That's not the way it works now," says Ron. "That's the way it worked when you were a child. Your mother was terribly intrusive and demanding. She always wanted to tell you what to do and how to do it. She felt like an ogre to you; huge, dominating, frightening. Through your anger work you have shoved her out of that position and felt your own power. But if you stay with your anger, you must keep seeing her as potentially a dangerous monster. It is only when you really see the scared and hurt child within her—a child who holds no terrors for you—that you can know that you have no reason ever to be afraid of her again."

"But if I forgive her, how can I stop her from walking all over me?" asked Arnold.

"What do you mean by 'walking all over you'?"

"Saying insulting things, making all sorts of demands."

"When you have forgiven her, you can reject her insults and refuse her demands from a position of caring and strength, rather than letting them enrage you, and thereby becoming her victim all over again. When you go into a rage, you are letting her decide how you are going to feel. This is your life. You should be able to decide for yourself how you want to feel."

Cheryl wrote:

> *I began to understand what caused a sweet little baby to turn into such a punishing, angry woman. I saw a pretty little girl with long red hair living on a farm with a harsh, cruel, and unfeeling mother and an uninvolved, compliant, invisible father. She was the oldest child and practically had to raise her seven younger brothers and sisters, doing back breaking amounts of hard labor. Her mother believed that there was virtue in doing things the hard way, and never let up on her. She had responsibilities that should never have been placed on the shoulders of a little girl.*
>
> *I was finally able to see her small child's face, the eyes reflecting absolute terror, and brimming with tears. I was able to let this poor frightened, dirty child climb up on my lap and be held and embraced. I felt that I could accept what happened when she was grown up and became my mother.*

Forgiveness for parents leads to a renewed connection to everything that was good in childhood. And with that connection with our parents, the compassion and understanding and love we feel for them can be felt more clearly for ourselves.

Judy, who had felt all her life that her mother somehow abandoned her by dying when she was six, wrote:

> *The great thing for me is that I've learned what our childhoods were really like. I feel like I've got all this information, this picture of what happened to both of us. I'm not afraid to look anymore. It's hard to explain what effect that has on me, but it's really important. There is a photo album at home*

118

> *that I've actually never looked at. I took it down and I finally felt okay looking at the pictures of me when I was little, and of my mother and father. I could feel sad for those three lost little children.*

They were told to ask the child of their mother how she learned specific patterns. Charlie wrote that his child had asked:

> *Why did you teach me that we were so much smarter and better than everybody else? That one really messes up my ability to get to know people and have friends.*

His mother's child answered,

> *Because it was all I had. Mom and Dad were proud of me because I did real well in school, but they didn't love me or even pay much attention to me for anything else. I didn't get to have pretty clothes, and I wasn't any good at sports, and the other kids at school didn't like me much. The only thing I had that made me feel good was that I was smarter than they were and that made me better than them.*

His child began to see her in a different light. After his questions about many other patterns were answered, he could say:

> *I'm sorry, Mary. I feel sad that you had such a painful childhood. I'm not surprised that you see life the way you do and that you behave the way you do. You didn't have any choice. That was the only way you could survive.*

Finding full compassion

Forgiveness of our parents must be as heart-wrenchingly deep an experience as our anger at them has been. Understanding how our parents came to be the way they are is preliminary, but not enough, for the full experience of forgiveness. It is only when the real emotional connection is made that the love which is always latent—because we were born wanting to love and be loved—can again be freed.

After the members have reached a state of understanding and compassion for their mothers' childhoods, a special session brings them to a deeper level of feeling, to the freedom of real forgiveness.

They are asked to bring in materials to set up a small individual altar, a white cloth, a candle, and an object or two that symbolizes their mothers to them. Charlie brings a loaf of freshly made bread, because his mother liked to bake. Cheryl brings a copy of a book of poetry her mother loved and read to her when she was little. Others bring pieces of jewelry their mothers had given them, or other decorative items. Many of them bring photographs.

When they are each seated in front of the little altar they created and the candles are lit, Dorothea talks to them about the experience they are about to have.

She reminds them how wonderful it was to discover their own strength and power in these past weeks, as they fought through to victory and freedom. They have come to know and appreciate themselves more deeply than they ever have. Now, however, the child within them may be afraid that they will have to give up some of this new sense of themselves if they truly forgive their mothers. She assures them, however, that real understanding and compassion for themselves or for anyone else comes out of a sense of inner strength, never from weakness. Opening their hearts to their mothers will only further empower them.

Dorothea suggests that they take a moment to look with honesty at some of the things they have done and the people they have hurt, and ask themselves whether they, too, are in need of compassion and forgiveness.

"For it is only in forgiving her that you will be able to find real forgiveness for yourself," she says. "Think of the pain and sorrow you have experienced in your own life, and remember how much pain and sorrow there has been in your mother's life. Be willing to admit to yourself the desire for revenge that has been hidden within you all of these years. It has been poisoning your life; be willing to let the sweet fullness of your compassion for her cleanse it out."

She leads them into visualizing the sanctuaries within their minds, serene and spacious and beautiful, with their magnificent guiding spirits present. They are to go to a special place, where they will to see a very important scene with their mothers. "Whether your mother is still living or not," she tells them, "let yourself accept this

120

scene as being real right now."

She tells them to picture themselves walking all alone in a deserted cemetery at dusk, watching the shadows among the tombstones. Then, with a sudden thud in their hearts, they each find themselves standing before a tombstone that bears, clearly engraved, the name of their mother. In the shock of recognition, a flood of memories open, and they relive the time of her death.

She goes on to describe how they see themselves receiving the sudden phone call informing them that their mother has been taken to the hospital in critical condition, and how they rush there in a state of shock and confused agitation, desperately hoping that she will not die until they can talk with her for one last time. She brings them to their mother's bedside, alone with her in the hospital room, seeing her age and frailness, hearing her labored breathing.

"No matter what your relationship has been like since you grew up, all memories of resentment and withholding fade as you realize that she is dying," her soft voice continues. "Your memories of the moments you had together when you were little come flooding back. You want so desperately for her to recognize you, to be able to connect with her in a real way before it's too late."

By this time many of the group are weeping; all are hushed and turned inward. Dorothea gives them time to feel the poignancy of the scene, and then to see the eyes of an innocent little girl gazing up at them from the face of the aged and tired and unfulfilled woman in the hospital bed. They see her recognize them gladly and tearfully. They hear her whisper how much she had wanted to give them a loved and happy childhood, how much grief and remorse she feels because she hadn't known how, and how much she wanted things to be different between them.

Dorothea gives them time to say from their hearts all that they want to tell their mothers. As she takes them deeper and deeper into the sense of grief and loss they are experiencing, she suggests words they might want to use. "Mother, please listen to me. I want you to know I'm not angry anymore. I know now that you couldn't help what you did, that it was only what you had learned. I just wish so much that we could have some time together to love each other at last."

They hear their mother, still caught up in her remorse over the past, saying over and over, "I'm sorry. I wanted it to be better. I just didn't know how. I'm so sorry, so sorry."

As they sense her slipping away, they can feel their desperate desire to let her know that they had let the unhappiness of the past go. They can touch her hands and stroke her forehead, and wipe her tears away. They can feel her respond to the love in their touch and their words and let go of her anguish. They see a tender, peaceful little smile come over her face as she dies.

Dorothea then takes the group through the scenes of the funeral, giving them another chance to feel deeply the process of letting go and saying goodbye.

Alicia wrote:

> *I can tell by her look that she still isn't sure if I'm here because of duty or because I really love her. She knows I've had something against her for a long time, and I don't think she even knows what it is.*
>
> *All I can think to say is, "I'm so sorry for all the loving times we didn't have together. I want you to know how much you mean to me. How much I love you. And I know you've always cared a lot about me. We just didn't know how to say it to each other." I feel her hand holding mine a little tighter and I start sobbing.*
>
> *Then her eyes close, and I can tell she's dead. My stomach is full of knots. I don't really believe it—it seems impossible. "I forgive you, Mom. Please forgive me. I never meant to cause you so much pain. Neither of us knew how to love each other."*
>
> *Afterwards, at the funeral, I keep sobbing. I want to hold her, to reassure her, to comfort her. And somehow I have the feeling that I'm doing this, that it is still possible. As she is lowered into the grave, I say, "Go in peace, Mom. Rest easy. I love you." And still the tears keep flowing, because even as I let her go I feel an emptiness in my heart.*

But then I'm back in the meeting room and I pick up a photograph I brought of Mom. I put it next to the candle so I can see her better, and the candle is reflected in her face. I know that her soul burns brightly inside her like that, and that there is great beauty in her that sometimes shows through.

As I write this, I feel a lot of hopes for my mother's and my relationship. Though the pain of our tragedy hasn't gone away yet, it isn't like a pain of anger or of hurt anymore. I think it is the pain of the compassion that I feel for both of us now.

Tom's notes said:

I felt frightened by how realistic the sense of my mother dying was for me. I felt that she was finally completing her whole self-destruction, and I had a very familiar sense of loneliness and fear. Throughout the visualization I felt bursts of emotion—sadness, fear, emptiness, longing, grief— and then periods when my intellect would get back in control, and I'd feel very little.

What really hit me hardest was when Dorothea described my child looking down into the grave at her casket and saying, "I'm letting you go, Mommy." That really struck a chord inside of me. I felt like, "No, I don't want to let go yet. How can I let go when I never had you? I'm not ready. It's not fair. It hurts. Mommy, come back . . ." And I cried, tears coming from way down deep. Old pain, present pain, even some new pain of recognizing that I never did have my mother.

Angie wrote of her experiences the next day:

I felt that letting go of my anger at my mother would leave me hollow and empty, but what's true is I felt very full, alive, still, and peaceful inside. It's not that anger is not going to come again, it's that it did not shatter me to let it go. I can bend like the willow. I can feel compassion without feeling responsible or guilty, and it leaves me feeling deeper and

123

*purer. Mother and grandma's lives were and are sad, but it
is not my responsibility, and I have a freedom of choice they
did not see that they had. I felt wonderful.*

How it really was for father

After the work with mother is complete, it is time to explore
father's childhood, and come to an understanding of what caused
father to behave as he did.

As a preliminary, Ron talks again about forgiveness as consciously
letting go of anger and resentment. He reminds the group that they
have found that they can be big enough to both explore their own
pain and anger, and to see another person's plight. "You will never
be able to see your father as another human being," he warns them,
"if you try to hold on to the relationship you had with him when you
were a child."

"But I am still going to think that what he did stinks," says Elaine
firmly.

"Absolutely," Ron agrees. "To feel compassion for him is not to
condone his behavior anymore than your mother's, or to try to
convince yourself that it was right. It is only to understand fully, so
you can let go of your own resentment and bitterness. Then you will
be open to the possibility of a new relationship with him in your mind
and also out there in physical reality, if he is still living."

Peter's description of his talk with his father's child read in part:

*Peter's child: How did you learn to be so withdrawn and
unfeeling? I was just a little kid, and I wanted you to love me
so much!*

*Father's child: I guess it was because I never felt that my
father cared about me. He was cold and unemotional and
inflexible. I guess I was just acting like him.*

*Peter's child: That's not enough excuse! Why didn't you
remember how bad he made you feel, and not do the same
thing to me? You made me feel rotten and worthless!*

*Father's child: I don't know. It was like I couldn't see that.
Once when I was about eight years old my father saw my*

124

mother giving me a hug, and he yelled at her not to make me a worse sissy than I was already. I felt her arms around me drop away, and I felt so unprotected and alone, standing there in front of my father. He never paid any attention to me except to criticize me and tell me how worthless I was. I think I learned that that was the way fathers are.

In his imagery, Peter kept demanding more and more answers. His father's child gradually showed him a childhood as deprived of a father's affection and support as his had been, with the addition that his father's mother was sickly throughout most of his childhood, and died when he was nine. Father's child described how his father's drinking and open womanizing and disinterest in his children had gotten even worse after that. After many pages of such dialogue, Peter's child was able to see things differently:

Peter's child: I think I understand how you learned to be the way you were. You just didn't have any way to learn to be different. I'm sorry your life was so hard, Dad. I really am sorry.

Father's child: I'm sorry, too, Pete. I know you didn't deserve the way I treated you when I grew up and became your father.

In Angie's notes, she asked her father about the way he had learned to be harsh and punishing toward his children and such a wimp toward his wife, and heard him tell of the cruelty of his own childhood. Then she suddenly turned to the central issue.

Child: But, how the hell could you do what you did to me? How could you molest your own daughter? How could you destroy my life that way?

Father's child looks down, hesitates, and seems to shrink: I still don't understand that whole thing, and I hate to think about it. I knew it was wrong, but somehow I couldn't stop. My father did it to me, too. Most of the time he just treated me like dirt, and I was terribly afraid of him, but sometimes in the fields or in the barn he'd be real nice when he wanted to—to use me sexually. That was the only time anybody ever

125

touched me and made me feel loved and important when I was a kid.

Angie's child: But you made me think I was bad, and I was making you do it, and that everybody would think I was a nasty wicked girl if I told anyone!

Father's child: Yeah, I know I did that. I was terrified that you would tell your mother, or someone else. He did that to me, too. He threatened me. I was afraid he'd kill me if I told anyone.

Angie's child (thoughtfully): It sounds as if the same things you did to me really did happen to you. And maybe you did feel the same way I did.

It is the beginning of understanding for Angie. The groundwork has been laid. She will need to do a lot more work with Dorothea in private sessions, however, before she is able to let go of her rage at what her father did to her and be free to move on in her life.

Everyone in the group puts in many hours talking in imagery with their fathers, tracking each major item of negative behavior and attitude back to its roots in their father's childhood. Gradually, they once again understand that what they had suffered in their childhoods was part of an ongoing history, and that their fathers were no more guilty than their mothers.

The group session

At the next meeting, Peter says, "I was thinking about cleaning up my relationship with my father and it scared me, because it means I will have to be the one who is the parent and in control. I know if I confronted him in person about our lives together—or rather our lives apart—he'd just deny it. So I'd have to handle all these patterns that we've entwined our lives with. I'd have to get to be a saint."

"You might have to get to be yourself," Marion suggests.

"I might, all right," Peter agreed. "But it's one thing to be my own self here in this room, it's another thing to go home for the holidays and be my own self in front of my father."

"But you could start," Marion tells him. "And you don't have to do it perfectly. If you don't give yourself permission to not do it perfectly, you won't even start."

Arnold says. "I guess there will still be some pain in being with him, and I'll make some mistakes. But I don't have to give all my energy to stifling that pain by drinking or smoking dope or carousing like I used to. I have a whole lot of other things I'm good at that I could be doing instead."

"Good for you," Ron says. "You're starting to take your own life more seriously."

Letting father go

The next session is focused on moving the compassion and understanding of their fathers to the same level of emotional conviction the group members have reached with their mothers. The experience of death can open the way to a deep acceptance of the value of life, as well as its fragility. They all will take their lives more seriously as they get a deeper sense of the reality of the loss of loved ones, and the pain of a life that had been unfulfilled and unlived.

The candles are lit as the members sit once again before the altars they have created. Dorothea's expressive voice leads them to a doctor's office where their father is receiving the shocking and unexpected news of his imminent death. Ron takes over then, speaking for a man who had heard such terrible words and is trying to take them in. His thoughts turn to his children, and the deep sorrow he feels that he has not been a better father, that his children are not close to him, that his early dreams of a loving family life have not been fulfilled. He speaks about how he really feels toward his son or his daughter in the depth of his heart, and how unable he has been to express those feelings.

Dorothea takes them through the scene of his death then, with the members of the group given time to speak to him, to comfort him, to truly connect with him for this one last time.

It is a long visualization. Eventually, Dorothea takes them slowly through the funeral itself, step by step. Some of the group are sobbing loudly; all are deeply involved. Kathy puts her hand quietly on Charlie's shoulder, glad that a few tears are sliding down his cheek, knowing that being touched sometimes helps him to go deeper into his feelings.

Afterwards, they spend a couple of minutes looking at and handling the momentoes of their fathers, remembering. They are invited then to talk with the person next to them about their feelings on having just come from their father's funeral. The murmured voices are warm and tender, punctuated with a few sobs and soft laughter as they share good memories of their fathers, and loving thoughts about him. As they speak, they come back into connection with each other, and with the present.

In her notes about the session, Lily wrote about the father who had paid so little attention to her and had died ten years ago:

> *When I smelled the apple I had put next to his picture, it brought back the apple tree in our backyard that he tended so carefully, and I remembered the joy he took in his garden, and I thought of how he was always building something, and how he took us on hikes in the mountains, and to fairs, and how he seemed to know how to do everything.*
>
> *When Dorothea talked about how at his death he wanted someone to know that he had lived, I felt a sort of anguish that people might forget him. And I thought about how he had given me life, and how he was so pleased with me sometimes, and that I have been able to step toward freedom from the bitterness that he lived and died with. And I felt that I have so much to live for. I felt like I belonged to myself, but that I also belonged to him in a spiritual way, and that that is a source of courage and strength for me.*
>
> *At his graveside, I talked to my father for a while, telling him that I would remember him, and that I was grateful for the gift of life. And I told him how sad I was that the innocent, beautiful child he had been had to endure so much pain that his life would be filled with bitterness and resentment. And I told him some of the good things I remembered about him. I told him I knew he was happy that I was freeing myself from generations of pain, and that his grandson was*

going to be okay because I was learning to be a different kind of mother.

I asked him if he wanted to say anything to me. Comforting thoughts filled me and I can't remember what they were, but they were good and strong and they made me feel strong. I felt as if they were his gift to me.

Ann wrote:

I stared at the photograph I'd put on my altar, seeing my father as such a young boy, a frightened boy inside a man's body, feeling lost, helpless, and desperately struggling to maintain control over the world for fear of losing it all. Tears came to me in waves. I felt so moved by the thought of him actually dying and leaving me. How sad it was—and how unexpected. I've always felt as if he would always be there. But it felt right to open to feeling the fear and grief of the other possibility—which is the truth. I was able to admit then that the real loss of my father happened a long time ago—and I've been looking for him ever since.

So what was most important to me in this session was the sense that in finding compassion for my father and for myself, I was finding myself. And even if I continue to search for him now and again, I know that one day I'll give it up and come home to myself for good.

Mike's notes read:

As I talked to Dad on his deathbed, I felt the pain of his life having been so afraid, angry, and lonely. I told him that I love him and forgive him, and I cried more deeply and freely than I think I ever have. I got a taste of what it will feel like to really lose him, and I decided that I will behave differently with him and express my love toward him more openly and strongly, and not wait for a real deathbed scene, which is a chance I might not even get.

As Kathy suggested, I also talked with Mother again and felt the same strong compassion (and cried some more) for her having felt unloved and unlovable, and the same resolution to treat her differently while she is still alive.

I said good-bye then, and saw myself walking away. I felt calm and free and ready to live.

Chapter Eight Exercises

Ask yourself these questions and note the answers in your journal or put them on tape.

Exercise 1

This exercise should be done separately for your mother (and mother substitutes) and for your father (and father substitutes).

a. Imagine that you are sitting down with your mother, not as you have known her, but when she was a child. Remember the negative traits she was demonstrating in the scene about which you confronted her. Imagine asking her child how she learned that behavior from her parents.

b. Imagine that she tells you openly and honestly and without defensiveness what she learned from her mother and father. If she was hostile in the scene, she learned to be that way from one or both of her parents, if she was anxious, or withholding, or smothering, she learned that, too. If there is something about that scene your child doesn't understand, or needs more clarification about, ask your mother's child to explain more. Let your guiding spirit help your child remain open and genuine, not angry or bitter or defensive.

Remember that understanding how your mother came to be the kind of person she did does not invalidate what you have learned about your negative experiences in childhood. Continue the conversation with her until you have a real sense of what it was like for her as a child. In the story of her childhood you can find the basis of understanding and compassion for her.

c. Can you see that your mother was doing in that scene what her parents trained her to do? Can you see that she was not to blame?

You are only being asked to experiment with a single scene for each of your parents, in order to have a sense of what actually happened in your life and in theirs. There were, of course, many other scenes and many other negative traits and behaviors.

Exercise 2

After you have completed Exercise 1 to your satisfaction, find a quiet time and place where you won't be disturbed for half an hour. Sit down before a picture of your mother, or some small object that symbolizes her in your mind. Close your eyes and take half a dozen or more deep, slow breaths.

Now continue the slow, regular breathing, and with each out-breath repeat to her silently, "I send you my good will," continuing for half an hour. You need add nothing to that statement, just letting yourself be aware of whatever feelings are arising in you, accepting whatever comes and letting it be. This simple exercise can help bring about a major shift in your feelings about your mother.

Exercise 3

Repeat Exercises 1 and 2 for your father (and any mother and father substitutes you may have had).

Exercise 4

After you have completed this work for both your mother and your father (and any substitutes), take another half an hour at a separate time to sit quietly and repeat the sending of good will, this time to yourself and your own inner child.

Stage IV: Integration

Chapter Nine: Being in Charge

Letting go

There are several more important sessions after the group finishes the anger and the forgiveness work. The members need to solidify their forgiveness of both their parents and themselves. They need to continue valuing their emotions and their spiritual natures. They need to integrate what they have learned, and to experiment with the shape their lives will take after the course is over.

Now that the grip of emotional dependency on their parents is broken, their negative patterns are becoming workable. The members are learning that they can choose their reactions instead of letting them be chosen by their parents. They are beginning to see things more objectively. Again and again, the teachers encourage them to realize that their aim is to become more and more authentic, not to become perfect. They need to recognize themselves as the architect in charge, not of a completed project, but of building their lives.

Ron tells them, "To take charge of our lives, we have to be willing to take responsibility for them. The definition of responsibility I like is 'the ability to respond for yourself—not for your parents—to whatever happens.'

"One way of responding for ourselves is to be willing to take responsibility for the situations we are in," he says. "We have done a lot of work on recognizing the way we were set up to get ourselves into negative situations. Now, though, we've got to be willing to look at what we are still doing to keep ourselves in them. If we are in a relationship or a job we don't like, we can start questioning, 'What are the choices I am making that are keeping me here?' When we were children, we learned to make some choices that have not been good for us. Because of that, we may be in situations we don't like. But, our lives will make more sense to us if we become aware of how we are contributing to being where we are."

He goes on to make the point more specific. "For instance, if you always wind up with people who are critical of you, you can begin to investigate how that happens. You might decide that the world is filled with nastily critical people. The other possibility is that you might realize that there are some very critical people in the world—and you keep ending up with them. That second way of looking at it will empower you to explore what programmed behavior you are living out that keeps you involved with these people.

"Remember, we are not bad or guilty for being wherever we are. We have only made some bad choices. As we become freer from our childhood programming, we can begin to make some better ones."

Brad says, "Sometimes I don't know how to change things. I spent so much time on my homework this week that I didn't pay enough attention to my wife. She got mad and laid a real guilt trip on me. I wasn't sure what to do about that."

Ron agrees that some situations can't be changed overnight, and brings in another basic concept. "Figuring out how you got yourself into a particular situation, and learning how to make other choices, sometimes takes a while," he said. "But you can begin taking responsibility for your reactions to what is happening right away. You say she laid a guilt trip on you. Another way of thinking about it is that your wife expressed her disappointment with you—and you chose to feel guilty about it. I imagine you feel guilty a lot. Who did you learn that from?"

"Mostly from my mother."

"Right. And now that you don't have to continue feeling guilty to please your mother anymore, you have a choice about how you respond to what anyone else does. Most of us believe that our feelings are the inevitable result of someone else's actions. 'My girlfriend broke a date, so I got depressed.' 'My boss was acting like a jerk again this morning, so I got pissed off.' But now you have a choice. You can go back to the old ways you learned to react in order to protect yourself, or you can be open to a new possibility. When you recognize that you can actually choose how you are going to respond, you begin to own your own life."

Later in the session, the subject of continuing anger comes up. Even though they were deeply moved by the compassion work, Larry and Angie are not ready to experience forgiveness for both their parents. Ron tells them, and the group, "You are all different, and a lot of different things happened to you, so there are all kinds of choices you can make. You may decide that you still need your anger to stay in contact with your strength. You can grant yourself that right. You even may feel that your anger toward the negative images you carry of your parents still demands full and genuine expression; in that case, you can accept that reality and work with your pillow and bat as long as you need to.

"Someday, you may decide, though, to simply let your anger go. You also have that ability. We've all had experiences like that when we had a fight with someone we cared about. We were really angry for a while, and then at some point we knew that we were finished, and ready to go on."

Judy is worried. "But what if you do let the anger go and it comes back again later on?"

"Then you may have to do some more anger work," Ron says, "and also more compassion work when you are done with the anger. But understand that you can decide when you want to stop and do something different."

He asks them to grasp their hands together and pull hard. After a moment he says, "Notice the painful tension in your wrists and arms, and how it spreads into your shoulders and throughout the rest of your body. Now how are you going to get out of this difficult situation?" A ripple of laughter runs through the group as, one after another, they simply unclasp their hands.

Ron grins. "Think about living, chronically holding a stress position like that. Can you see how much energy it takes? That's what happens when you hold on to negative thoughts and emotions.

Holding on might feel safer because the old ways are so familiar, and we're always tempted to go back to what is familiar. But look what that stress does to your comfort and peace of mind.

"We've been learning that when we decide that we don't want to live like that anymore, we can change it. We can trace how we learned any reaction we are having and choose to re-image it. Then we can let it go, and begin to try out some new behavior.

"And I know only too well that new behavior is not always easy. Remember learning to drive a car? For a while when I was learning, I felt like I couldn't tell my left foot from my right one. Whenever we try to acquire a new skill, there is always a period when we are not terribly graceful. But being willing to go through the awkwardness of doing something new is a sign that we are moving and growing."

Ron reminds the group that they also may find themselves hanging on to old patterns, because newness in itself is frightening. "If you haven't been in a situation before, you don't know what the rules are. Most of us were taught as children to automatically be afraid of anything unknown. When we allow ourselves to move through our fears, though, we can begin to see new opportunities rather than old threats."

Reclaiming the good in childhood

The teachers now introduce a new element. For most of the members of the group, their early negative experiences had blocked out their memories of everything that was good about childhood. The very idea of a "happy childhood" was a mockery. Now, however, without denying the reality of all the destructive things that happened, they can reclaim the parts of their childhoods they hadn't been able to appreciate before.

The members have come to know their parents in a new way through the compassion and forgiveness that followed the anger work. Now they also can see their childhood years in a new way. They are asked to write about positive interactions with their mothers and fathers when they were young, and to give their parents credit for all that was valuable that they learned from them.

This is another gratifying and often deeply emotional stage in the

Process. The group members begin to remember the rich smells, excitement, and kindly intentions of Christmases and other holidays during their childhoods. They see that their mother's long hours spent in the kitchen, and their father's immersion in work, were also ways of taking care of them. They recognize valuable qualities they learned from their parents, like a love of nature, sociability, or an appreciation of music and art. Even those with almost totally irresponsibile or uncaring parents now see a more rounded picture.

Elaine wrote about the parents who had beaten her, and taught her such deep hostility:

> *I can see how I learned lots of my strengths from my parents. Much of the determination and courage that have served me so well in my life came from both of my parents, especially my mother who struggled so valiantly in the world. I learned how to function in almost any kind of environment and hold my own almost anywhere. I learned to be articulate from my parents, and to feel that I had a right to do anything I wanted to do.*

Of his critical and rejecting father, Peter wrote:

> *I remember the care my father took of me when I had a serious ear infection. He was so worried that I might lose my hearing. The doctors said that I needed surgery, but that it would be a very risky operation and my eardrum might be affected. My father took me to several specialists and found one who treated me without surgery. And sure enough, I got better. If it hadn't been for my father, I might not be able to hear today.*

Opening herself to memories of the times her often angry and impatient stepfather had shown his capacity for kindliness, Cheryl wrote:

> *One particularly vivid memory is when I was waiting by the side of a stream for my Dad to quit fishing because it was getting dark. I heard him swear suddenly. He had a bat caught in his hook. The more the poor thing thrashed around, the more tangled it was becoming. I could hear its*

high-pitched sounds as it struggled to get free. I was so shaken I could hardly hold the flashlight still for him to see what he was doing. I kept screaming, "Don't kill it, Daddy, don't let it die!"

This was a situation in which my father could easily have lost his temper. Instead, he calmly told me he was doing everything he possibly could, and he didn't want the bat to die either. I got more frantic by the minute, but he didn't freak out at me or at the situation. Finally, after at least fifteen minutes, he was able to set the bat free. I yelled, "Daddy, you did it, you saved the bat! Yeah for Daddy!" I was so proud of him, both for saving the bat and for not getting mad at me. He really came through on that one.

Margie, too, could see another side of her mother.

When my father got sick, my mother had to go out and learn how to make a living. Not many women did that in those days, so it took tremendous strength and courage. But she did it, and she never lost sight of the family. She still spent time with us in the evenings and on weekends, and sometimes we even went on holiday trips. From having no skills outside the home, my mother learned office work and eventually became office manager and indispensable to her employer. She was very organized at home, too. People would come and ask for help, and she always gave it. I remember looking at my mother's hands one day. They were pale, with the veins showing. They looked like they worked hard. There was a nice feeling about them. I wanted to have hands just like hers.

Alicia remembered a sweet early memory.

I'm surprised at how readily these scenes are coming back! I see my father coming to me in the kitchen where I've been watching Mommy cook. He picks me up in his arms and carries me down the steps to the basement. I get to help him fix the water heater. He's explaining everything to me. I get to hold the tools for him and I'm only three years old! I

138

remember calling him "honey" that day. That's what my mom calls him and they laugh when I call him that. I say it because I love him.

Kathleen went back to moments when she had felt part of her mother's world when she was little, and how important that had been to her.

When Mommy was going out she would let me help her get dressed. I would get to find the right pair of shoes and sometimes pick out the earrings I wanted her to wear. And then I would stand on the bed and do up her zipper. Mommy looked so pretty and I was so glad she was my Mommy.

Tom could see another side of his father's anxieties:

My Dad worried a lot, but that's not what he meant to teach me. In the best ways he knew how, he tried to prepare me for a world that he saw as very dangerous. He often would try to get me to think about what I wanted to do when I grew up, and he kept a close check on how I was doing in school. He was truly concerned and expressed as much. Even as a child, I knew he was showing his love for me that way. And even though I rebelled and quit school, my career is important to me, and I'm going back to college this fall.

Charlie summed up the new mood in the group.

To be able to see, appreciate, respect and accept the strengths and good things I learned from my folks without having to rebel against them, or blame myself for having felt so bad anyhow, is a powerfully positive and validating experience. I'm happy and proud to be reclaiming them and celebrating being the child of my parents.

Creating our own lives

At another session, Ron tells the group, "Up to now, your life has been controlled largely by old shadows and old fears, your destiny has been determined by your parents. All the work we have been doing is so that you can begin to create your own destiny. But that still isn't going to be easy. What do you see that could stop you from being a powerful, authentic, loving adult?"

The members of the group know that as they genuinely bring what they have learned into their lives they will not be the people they used to be. The prospect of radical change brings up old anxieties. They are quick with answers: "It's possible that everyone won't like me." "I'd have to be responsible for the things I do, nobody else." "I don't know how to do it, I haven't had models." "I feel like I don't deserve it." "It goes against everything I've been trained to believe about myself."

Ron agrees. "All of that is true. For our whole lives, we've been trained to see ourselves as small and weak, as somebody's hopeful or rebellious child. And, of course, there are some advantages in continuing to be a child. Someone else can be the authority, which means we don't have to be responsible for ourselves. We get to be taken care of, or else we get to blame other people and complain about not being taken care of.

"We learned to trade freedom for safety when we were small, to submit to control and to seek approval. And many of us are still doing that. Even if we rebel, it's still a child's rebellion, intended to keep us in connection with whomever we are rebelling against. Some of us live our whole lives trying to make our mates, bosses, friends and the organizations that we work for into our parents so we'll feel safe.

"To grow up into full maturity means at times to live with tension and anxiety. Much of what grown-up human beings do feels risky. We find that it is difficult at times to speak the truth, to own our own part, to feel our own pain, to acknowledge our own remorse, to experience our own sorrow, to accept that we won't always know for sure, and to be our own authority.

"Many of us feel like children in our work, for instance. We wait for the organization to tell us what to do and how to do it, and to make us feel good. And many bosses willingly act the part of parent. They will reward us, punish us, and set our goals. If we are good enough and nice enough, somebody will make everything okay for us. Do any of you recognize that pattern?"

There are murmurs of assent from the class and someone murmurs, "Painfully."

Ron nods. "It is painful, isn't it? And not submitting to being taken over like that doesn't mean being hostile and rebellious. It means not being willing to give our lives away because we've been taught that somebody else knows what is good for us better than we do.

"If we want freedom, if we want our own lives back, no one else can give it to us. We cannot be somebody's child. We can have childlike qualities, but we cannot continue to be children. It isn't easy to be a mature and compassionate adult. There would be more people free, if it were easy. But what you have been doing in the weeks you have been here has not been easy. It has taken commitment and hard work. You have earned every step you have gained, and with each step you've reclaimed more and more of your own life. Now the next steps are up to you."

The members of the group listen quietly. Their Process is drawing to a close. Much gladness and good fellowship and appreciation is expressed in these last meetings, but the members also recognize that they are being challenged to move on.

"In truth, you are eagles," Ron tells them. "But at this point, you have just broken out of the shell. The fact that you have broken out does not mean that you know how to take care of yourself perfectly, or that you have developed into your full strength and beauty and are now ready to soar. It means that you are out of the shell! Now there are possibilities. You can learn. You can choose.

"You will discover much joy and much freedom in your life after the Process. Remember, though, it is often when we stand up to what frightens or enrages us—when we allow our experience to deepen and find the strength to go through it—that our lives are most rich. Knowing that we can stand fast for ourselves changes our anxiety over what is going to happen next to excitement and eagerness. Instead of looking for safety, we can risk. Instead of being controlled or controlling others, we can be partners with others. Instead of seeking approval and giving ourselves away for it, we can love and cherish and respect all that lives within us."

141

Chapter Nine Exercises

Ask yourself these questions and note the answers in your journal or put them on tape.

Exercise 1

a. Remember a time when you were angry at someone you cared about, and eventually let go of the anger and went back to being friends. What happened to make that possible?

b. Think about the people you've known who are mostly angry, resentful and vindictive. How does the quality of their lives feel to you?

c. Think about the people you've known who are mostly genuinely kind and generous. How does the quality of their lives feel to you?

d. What would your life be like if you were able to experience yourself as a complete individual, separate and autonomous from your parents?

e. What would it add to the quality of your life if you were also able to be in a warm and mutually supportive relationship with them (to the extent that is realistically possible)? Even if they are dead it is possible to have such a relationship with your memories of them.

Exercise 2

a. Make a list of three of your mother's virtues and strengths and three of your father's virtues and strengths.

b. Write a paragraph for each of your parents, describing how those virtues and strengths have become a part of you.

Chapter Ten: **Afterwards**

A few months after they finish the Process, the group gathers together with the teachers to compare notes on how their lives are going. Many have become friends, of course, and see each other often. A number of the members are continuing to meet with their individual teacher/therapists to deal with issues that are surfacing in their everyday lives, as well as to work more deeply with some of their childhood material than was possible within the rapidly moving structure of the Process. There is great pleasure, however, in all of them being together again. After much hugging and laughter they settle down in the familiar room to report to each other and the teachers on their progress.

This is a time for the teachers to listen, and the members of the group to do the talking. After a little hesitation, Alicia begins. "Some of you know that my father died a week after the Process ended, and I've had a lot of pain around that. But before he died I had a chance to put my arms around him and hold him and tell him that I really loved him. He had been pretty much unconscious for days, but he opened his eyes and looked right at me and he said, 'Hi, sweetheart, I love you, too.' That was the last exchange we had. That was a tremendous gift. I never would have taken a chance like that before I did this work, and I never would have had that moment to remember."

Her voice quivers, and the women on either side of her touch her comfortingly. After a moment, she continues, "I wasn't there when he actually died. He was in a coma, and I went out for a long walk.

143

My Mom was mad at me for that, and she tried to make me feel guilty for not having stayed at the hospital. Before, I would have taken that to my grave. My sister thought I should be angry with her for talking to me that way, but I was able to say, 'It's okay. She's hurting a lot, that's all.' And I didn't carry it, and it's not with me now. I was really able to see her pain. I was hurting, too, but she had just lost the most significant part of her life. It was all built around him.

"For weeks after he died, there was a dialogue going on between my child, who just wanted to stay home and cry because her Daddy was gone, and my intellect, who didn't think that was a very mature way to handle it. That dialogue would never have happened before. My feelings would just have been shoved into a box and I would have gone on. I'm not behaving the way I once would have thought I should behave, but it feels all right to me. I'm being gentle with myself and giving myself time to grieve. And my mother and I have even gotten so we can cry together."

She smiles at them, almost shyly. The group is silent for a few moments, feeling her loss with her, glad for her moment of profound connection with her father, and the beginning connection with her mother.

Current relationships with parents are always on the agenda at these meetings. When the group completed the Process, Ron had advised them that they should go to their mothers and fathers, if it was possible, and reconstruct their relationships with them in the light of what they had discovered.

Ann is relaxed and smiling as she tells the group about her recent visit to her mother in her retirement home in Florida. "I've spoken to my mother only five times in the last ten years, so at first we were pretty stiff with each other. After I'd been there a couple of days, though, it was clear that whatever trouble had gone on between us was over.

"On the third day, I did what Marion suggested. I told her that I'd let go of the past, and that I loved her. I knew I needed to do that for myself. What really surprised me was her reaction. She's never been the emotional type, but she got tears in her eyes and her voice was shaking. She said that she'd missed me a lot, and that she loved me, too. All of a sudden, it seemed natural to hug her. I had tears in my

144

eyes, too.

"Since I got back, we've been talking on the phone, and she's coming out to visit me in a couple of months. I'm a little worried about how it will go, but not very much, because I feel pretty centered these days."

After a while, Mike said, "Well, my mother lives only ten miles from me, so I see her on holidays and family occasions. But I always tried to make my visits as short as possible, because they're never comfortable.

"After the Process, I sat down with her for about an hour and we talked. She started into one of her negative spins and I got a glimpse of myself as a kid, desperately wanting to make Mommy happy, or at least to get her out of this negative stuff.

"But this time, I just told her some of the things I learned in this work. I wasn't ready to tell her that I loved her, but I did tell her that what I learned was that the most important thing was for me to love myself, and then I'd be able to love my wife and my children, and the rest of my family. That kind of changed things. She said that she regretted a lot of things that happened between us, and I could tell she meant it.

"Ever since then, she doesn't direct the negative stuff at me anymore. She knows I'm a gardener, so now she gives me things for my garden, which is kind of nice. It's like we've got a common interest. I'm going to take her out to breakfast on Sunday. I never would have taken time to be with her like that before. We're actually getting to be friends."

As Larry tells the story of his interaction with his father, he seems more at peace than they've ever known him to be. "A few days after the end of the Process, I sat down with my father. I told him that he didn't have to say anything, I just wanted him to listen to me. He sat there looking at the wall. I told him how much I hated him during all the years that he was physically abusing me. I told him about the effect that has had on my life. I told him how much I was like him, and why I'd spent all those years being tough and hostile.

"I told him I was more than halfway through my life, and before I died, or he died, I wanted to tell him that I loved him. And all he needed to do was tell me one time that he loved me, because he'd never told me that. I was crying, I couldn't control it. He looked at me and he said, 'Well, Larry, I'm really glad that you spoke to me about this. I've thought about it a lot. When you kids came along, life was hard. I had to work two jobs, and it was rough. I admit I took it out on you. I know it doesn't help now, but I am really sorry I did that. And yes, I do want to tell you, I'm proud of you, and I do love you.' It just blew me away, because it never occurred to me that he'd felt guilty all this time, but he just couldn't tell me. I thought it was just great. And when I left him, I hugged him tight and he let me. I thought to myself, 'Even if I didn't do anything else in the Process, this one thing is worth it.'"

The group goes on to talk about other relationships and changes in themselves. Charlie tells them, "I lived with a woman for almost six years. We worked together, too, so I thought we knew each other pretty well. Since we split up we're still good friends, and one day last year she asked me how I was doing. I said, 'I'm a little depressed. I guess it is the same old self-doubt and lack of self-esteem.' She looked surprised and said 'You? Lacking self-esteem?' And I thought to myself, 'How could you live with me that long and not ever see the fear and anxiety in me?' I decided she was much more insensitive than I thought.

"I've come to realize, though, that it wasn't her fault if she didn't know me. I had such an elaborate and sophisticated cocoon built all around myself that nobody could know me. In these last months, I've been working hard at tearing that cocoon away chunk by chunk. I'm learning to be present in my life and in my relationships, instead of hiding like I've done in the past. I can see that it's working. It is difficult for me not to be optimistic about the future. I feel pretty good about it."

Tom is much more hesitant. "I didn't think that when the Process was over I would be happy all the time. But part of me was hoping that I would, and I'm not. I'm sometimes afraid that the fear, anger, and neediness I've lived with all my life will come rushing back. In fact, I've experienced moments of anger and not acting from a place of strength, especially when my boss pushes one of my buttons. I keep hearing some of the old messages, too.

"So, heaven didn't open up for me in the way I kind of hoped it would. But I'm beginning to appreciate the intimate nature of the changes I'm going through. What I notice most is a centered feeling, rather than feeling rushed and worried all the time. A lot of the time, when I've started to get upset, I've been able to trace my reactions back to the parent I learned it from and acknowledge it. Then I can let it go fairly easily."

"Sounds like an important shift," suggests Ron mildly. "The stages we go through are different for everybody. What matters is what happens to you, not whether it seems like more or less than is happening to anyone else. By the way, is there anyone here who hasn't had ups and downs, hasn't had some hard times?" Not a hand went up.

Diane had come into the Process overwhelmed with self-hatred. Tonight she says, "Before doing this work I felt very sad, very suicidal. I felt like no one could love a person like me. But I found out that the 'me' I hated was the 'me' I created according to somebody else's formula. The teachers and the Process introduced me to the real me, and I've come to realize that I'm pretty amazing! I found that I have strength and pride, and a lot of courage. I don't have to be perfect, I can just be me. I don't have to beat myself up for being human and making mistakes. For the first time in my life, I can say I love myself. That's an incredible accomplishment."

Glancing around, she adds thoughtfully, "It's been really painful to let go of the illusion that someone or something is going to come along and make my life what I always wanted it to be when I was a child, and to accept that nothing is going to happen unless I make it happen. But I've given up the idea that I need a protector to tell me what to do or to make me happy. I'm finding out that I really am responsible for my own happiness. It's been like discovering myself."

Peter leans forward and takes a deep breath. "I want to say something about that business of taking responsiblity, too. I met a woman from Holland a couple of weeks after the end of the Process, and we had a wonderful time together for almost a week before she had to go back home. Then a few days later, I suddenly started thinking that she might have had AIDS. The more I thought about it, the more terrified I got. I couldn't control the fear. I was so panicked that I could barely get myself out of the house to take a walk and try to calm myself down.

"After a while, I realized how the whole thing fit into my mother's catastrophic fears about illness and disease, and her injunctions against sex, and against taking risks of any kind. And though AIDS is deadly serious if you have it, the reality of the danger had nothing like the magnitude I was giving it. In my mind I said to my Mom: 'I took a risk. If I made a mistake, I will bear the consequences. It will be me who does that, not you.' And I began to feel that I was getting through the fear. I felt that I was taking charge again—that is, I as my child, my intellect, and my spirit, all together.

"I thought about how I had disobeyed my mother's ideas in even taking the Process. I was the one who decided to change my life, because I was deeply dissatisfied with the way it was. I took a risk with no guarantees. I did that, not my mother. And now, whether I live or die, it will be me who lives or dies, not my mother. It is my life now, it belongs to me, and I'm the one who has the responsibility for it!" He glances around, suddenly a little embarrassed at the profound conviction ringing in his voice. He is met with nods and a soft chorus of "yeah" and "right on."

Lily's voice is as soft as ever as she speaks. "Well, I don't know where my life is going right now. I've always been scared about lots of things. I'm still terrified about money. My firm is going through some changes, and I don't know what is going to happen to my job. And the house I live in has just been sold. I'm going to have to move, and I hate moving. So some parts of my life are like a nightmare right now. Sometimes, though, when I am struggling a lot, I realize that only the child part of me is terrorized and the spiritual part isn't. The spiritual part is able to put her arms around the child part and hold her and be strong and compassionate. That was one of the most important things for me during the Process—to realize that I can be scared and at the same time I can be compassionate and supportive toward myself."

Different members of the group nod soberly. It is a familiar experience to many of them. Kathleen sees her intellect as the wise part of her. "It's amazing to me," she says, "how often a nice voice pops in and says, 'be gentle, or be compassionate.' It's as if my

148

intellect has become a really neat coach, instead of telling my child how stupid and bad she is all the time. When I get into co-dependency stuff with my lover, the child gets scared a lot, and the intellect gently says, 'It's all right to feel that way, but let's have a reality check. You are not being left.' It is really quick and subtle, but it happens all the time."

Judy is next, "It's the same with me. I still find myself doing some things that I used to do. When I'm in a lot of pain, I'll create a fight with my husband, or sometimes I'll sit down and gorge myself. But now when that begins to happen, my intellect says, 'No, let's not do this right now, let's hang in for another couple of minutes.' Right away the pain my child is feeling begins to come up and I get to understand what's really troubling me. That way I can begin to deal with the real issues. I've gotten a lot more tolerant, not just of myself, but of other people. I'm more able to separate them from their patterns, just like I'm able to separate me from my patterns. That's one of the most profound changes in my life. I don't see myself as being my patterns anymore. My patterns are my patterns. They are not me. Who I am is still okay."

These descriptions of progress spark a detailed story from Cheryl about how she is learning to put what she found out about herself into action. "My boss said he wanted to discuss some of the office procedures with me. I got annoyed because I felt like I already understood them perfectly well. He told me to mellow out, that he just wanted to talk about it. Then he looked over at the bookkeeper and they both laughed. I felt like he was making fun of me, and I couldn't believe how hurt and angry I felt. I just wanted to scream at him.

"I ran off to the restroom because I was afraid I'd get really nasty and tell him off. But after I calmed myself down a little, I began to see how the whole scene was like the way my father treated me. He made me feel that I was causing the problems, being overly dramatic and emotional. He would joke about it and make fun of me. That's just what I felt that my boss was doing. I was seeing him through my father's glasses.

"After a while, I went back and just told him the truth about what I was feeling, and about why I felt that way. Saying that to him was kind of difficult, but it also felt like a new experience in letting someone see that I was being vulnerable and human. He was much more sensitive and caring than I thought he would be. He said he hadn't seen our interaction as a black mark against me, and that he was glad I told him how I felt. The whole thing about the office procedure became unimportant, and things have been a lot easier and friendlier between us ever since."

She hesitates and then admits, "Actually, I've been getting compliments on how much I have changed and how different I am. It feels really good, but I still get a little shaky hearing things like that—as if it would be spoiled if someone else noticed. I want to take it slow and get used to it."

Arnold has been sitting quietly, apparently deciding what he is going to say. Finally he speaks. "I don't know if I can say this, but, outside of the three months during the Process, I have been on dope and getting drunk a lot for ten solid years. When I told my girl friend about wanting to do the Process, she said I was looking for another quick fix and I should do regular therapy. But I said, 'My life is falling apart and I need something now. I'm not willing to wait for a year or two years or three.' I started in the Process and, for three weeks or four weeks, I watched what was going on and I thought, these guys are not for me. I really thought it was total bullshit. I thought you guys were out of your minds. But as the work went on I realized that it was fixing me. I'm off the dope, and the liquor, and I'm going to stay off."

"Who fixed you?" asks Kathy gently.

"I fixed me. Or rather, we fixed me."

"Maybe a better way to say it is that you are healing your self," she suggests. 'Fix' sounds like something needed to be fixed in you. I think that something needed to be honored in you, and now you are honoring it."

"Yeah," Arnold responds. "The evening I spent with some of the group after the final session was one of the best nights of my life. I was clear and very grounded and I felt wonderful. But after a few days, when things weren't so exciting anymore, I had a joint and a few beers. I decided that I just can't put my child through that anymore; it doesn't work. I joined Alcoholics Anonymous, and I'm going to stick with it.

150

"But what I really want to talk about is how really good I feel sometimes. I get into feeling down sometimes, too, but I don't have to believe it. The main thing I'm working on is learning to take care of myself, even though that's really hard for me to do. I have a vision of myself as being really healthy. I avoid it when I'm not feeling so good about myself, but I can see it when I'm clear."

Arnold, with his outspoken anger and humor, has been a favorite of the group from the beginning. Several, who knew about his history of addiction, are glowing with relief. Kathy grins at him. She knows he is putting into his recovery the same high energy that had gone into his rages at his angry and punishing stepfather, and she feels a lot of confidence in him.

Elaine leans forward. "It feels really good to hear all of this stuff. You know, I came into the Process pretty resistant and pretty arrogant. Mighty arrogant, as a matter of fact. I've taught courses in communication for a lot of my life, and I thought, 'Oh yeah, do these people really have anything they can teach me?' When you've been in the role of teacher for twelve years, it is really difficult to admit that the things you are teaching aren't working for you.

"After we started, and I felt so many of you showing caring and tenderness for me, it scared me. I did everything I could to try to make you go away. But you never gave up on me. Dorothea weathered all my storms, and when the clouds passed over she was still standing there, and so were the rest of you. That surprised me. I knew then that I had to find out why I isolated myself like that. If it hurt, it hurt, but I had to let someone in. I found I could allow a teacher to teach me, and to humble me—a little, anyhow. I could let her see me cry and tell me it was okay to learn how to do something.

"I found out I could let people love me, and love them back. So instead of fulfilling some pretty awful prophecies about myself that my parents instilled in me, like that I was going to die miserable and alone, I think I'm going to be all right."

Three of the group members are not in town for the meeting. Marion reads some paragraphs from their letters aloud to the group.

Angie had returned to Alaska. She wrote:

My greatest desire and passion all my life was to blame my parents and get my revenge. I wanted someone else to suffer as I have. If they weren't handy, anybody else would do. I knew it was a deadly, useless game, but I couldn't stop it.

Now I feel I am on the other shore after an incredible journey. I feel a tremendous sense of appreciation for my strength and courage not to deny the pain in my life; to see it, to understand it, to feel sadness and compassion for my mother, my father, and the little girl inside me who went through all those years of horror. I am not exhausted any longer from carrying around so much rage. I no longer feel that I will crumble and die when trouble comes. I have trust now that my patience will grow and I will know what is right for me in my life. I feel like finally I have really been born. I am strong and alive and I am learning how to grow myself up.

Brad was in Europe on business for his company. He wrote:

At times I didn't think I was ever going to blossom out of all the confusion I lived in during the Process, but I am feeling better about myself than I ever remember. I feel a lot more grounded, and clearer about how I feel and what I see. I am learning to say what I feel instead of invalidating my feelings as I used to. I am putting myself out into the world instead of holding back in fear of rejection. I feel more present and open to myself, which makes me here for others in ways I wasn't before. My son and I have a whole new relationship, and it's getting better all the time.

I still find myself falling back into some of the old patterns (and a few new ones I wasn't aware of before). But I'm not demanding perfection of myself; when pain or sorrow or anger come up I'm letting them teach me about myself. That seems to take me deeper into a sense of being more whole and real and alive. I am learning that I can be myself, and that is what I am letting myself be. And that is beautiful.

Margie was on an extended visit with relatives on the East Coast. She wrote:

The miserable black cloud I came in with was the weight of all the unfelt feelings, all the childhood hurts, the guilt, the shame, the unwelcomeness, the grief, the unexperienced love, the children I haven't had, the nieces and nephews I've ignored, the fear of saying the things that need to be said and doing the things that need to be done. The cloud is still there, but only when I am not.

How can I ever be bored or feel my life is over when there is so much I don't know about myself? Over for whom? Certainly not for my child who hasn't even been to South America or learned to paint yet. Certainly not for my spirit who has capacities for understanding and experience that are beyond my most extravagant dreams. To a life that was dark and empty, my work in the Process has brought connection with the depth and richness of my inner self and my potential for spiritual growth.

Chapter Ten Exercises

Ask yourself these questions and note the answers in your journal or put them on tape.

Exercise I

a. Create a dialogue between your child, your intellect, and your guiding spirit. What does each of them need to continue to flourish and unfold and grow?

For example, your child might say: I need to be able to express my emotions, to have opportunities to be creative, to have contact with nature, to have playmates and recreation, and most of all, to be listened to, loved, and accepted.

Your intellect might say: I need to become compassionate, protective and positive toward my child, to be discriminating not judgmental, to explore new options, to learn, to be able to freely use my best abilities.

Both need to recognize that the body needs to learn to relax, to be flexible, to dance, to be active, to get optimum rest and nourishment, to be in touch with itself.

Your guiding spirit might say: I need the support of a daily practice of meditation or visualizations, inspirational literature, wise teachers, a shared community, and most of all to be recognized and acknowledged by the rest of you.

b. Now create your own dialogue.

c. Are you willing to give each of them what they need?

The point of view of this book and of the Personal Change Process is that when we no longer have to recreate the old patterns, we are free to grow into the spontaneous, compassionate, able and knowing self we truly are, in loving connection with other human beings and with the world around us. A strong support to such continued personal and spiritual growth is the habit of looking at whatever we do with kind and gentle eyes instead of with the critical eyes of our parents and parent substitutes.

154

Endnote

For many years we have been deeply touched and heartened by the courage and love and wisdom—and the capacity for joy and power—that human beings evidence over and over again as they begin to free themselves from the learned belief systems and habitual responses that imprison them. With support and structure, and a framework in which to understand our experience, destructive and neurotic symptoms can fade away as something powerful and real and good within us begins to take over. We are intended for psychological and spiritual growth all of our lives, just as we grow physically when young.

There is also a wider significance to this work of freeing ourselves. In learning to love, appreciate, value, and care for ourselves, we become capable of truly loving, appreciating, valuing, and caring not only for our own families and friends, but for our neighbors throughout the world, and for the planet we all share.

The purpose of this book is to give you new insight into yourself and the possibilities that exist for you. To accelerate your own growth, though, it is necessary to deeply challenge your present behavior and attitudes and feelings, and your beliefs about yourself, your parents and your life. In doing this kind of work, therefore, it is most helpful to be guided by a knowledgable, skillful, and compassionate teacher or therapist who has done the work of healing with his or her own inner child.

For further information about the IPC Process itself, introductory workshops, and the IPC training program for teacher/therapists, please contact:

The Institute for Personal Change
2295 Palou Avenue
San Francisco, California 94124
(415) 550-6410.